MIRRORS AND LABYRINTHS

THE PROCESS OF A "NEW" AESTHETIC SYNTHESIS IN THE NOVELS OF JOHN BANVILLE

LAURA P. ZUNTINI DE IZARRA

International Scholars Publications
San Francisco - London - Bethesda
1999

Copyright © 1999, by
Laura P. Zuntini de Izarra

International Scholars Publications
4720 Boston Way
Lanham, Maryland 20706

12 Hid's Copse Rd.
Cumnor Hill, Oxford OX2 9JJ

All rights reserved
Printed in the United States of America
British Library Cataloging in Publication Information Available

Library of Congress Cataloging-in-Publication Data

Zuntini de Izarra, Laura P.
Mirrors and holographic labyrinths : the process of a "new" aesthetic synthesis in the novels of John Banville / Laura P. Zuntini de Izarra
p. cm.
Translation of the author's thesis written in Portuguese (doctoral—University of São Paulo, Brazil, 1995).
Includes bibliographical references and index.
1. Banville, John—Criticism and interpretation. 2. Postmodernism — Irish Literature. 3. Aesthetics, Modern—20th century. 4. Banville, John—Aesthetics. 5. Holography in literature. 6. Labyrinths in literature. 7. Mirrors in literature. 8. Metaphor. I. Title.

PR6052.A57Z9   1998   823'.914—dc21   98—33230 CIP

ISBN 1-57309-258-4 (cloth: alk. ppr.)
ISBN 1-57309-257-6 (pbk: alk. ppr.)

∞™ The paper used in this publication meets the minimum requirements of American National Standard for Information Sciences—Permanence of Paper for Printed Library Materials, ANSI Z39.48—1984

MIRRORS AND HOLOGRAPHIC LABYRINTHS

The Process of a "New" Aesthetic Synthesis in the Novels of John Banville

Laura P. Zuntini de Izarra

International Scholars Publications
San Francisco - London - Bethesda
1999

Library of Congress Cataloging-in-Publication Data

Zuntini de Izarra, Laura P.-
 Mirrors and holographic labyrinths : the process of a "new" aesthetic synthesis in John Banville's work / Laura P. Zuntini de Izarra
   p. cm.
 Translation of the author's thesis written in Portuguese (doctoral -- University of São Paulo, Brazil, 1995.
 Includes bibliographical references and index.
 ISBN 1-57309-258-4 (hardcover ; alk.paper)   -- ISBN 1-57309-257-6 (pbk. : alk.paper)
 1.Banville, John -- Criticism and interpretation. 2. Postmodernism (Literature) -- reland. 3.Aesthetics, Modern--20th century. 4. Banville, John -- Aesthetics. 5. Holography in literature. 6. Labyrinths in literature. 7. Mirrors in literature. 8. Metaphor. I. Title

PR6052.A57Z9 1998
823' .914—dc21   98-33230
                                                                      CIP

Copyright 1999 by Laura P. Zuntini de Izarra

All rights reserved. Printed in the United States of America. No part of this book may be used or reproduced in any manner whatsoever without written permission except in the case of brief quotations embodied in critical articles and reviews.

Editorial Inquiries:
International Scholars Publications
7831 Woodmont Avenue, #345
Bethesda, MD 20814
website: www.interscholars.com
To order: (800) 55-PUBLISH

Caminante, son tus huellas
el camino, y nada más;
caminante, no hay camino,
se hace camino al andar.
Al andar se hace camino,
y al volver la vista atrás
se ve la senda que nunca
se ha de volver a pisar.
Caminante, no hay camino,
sino estelas en la mar.

Antonio Machado,
 Proverbios y Cantares, XXIX

FOR Martín, Sebastián and Martín Ignacio,

    Santiago and Matías for accompanying us in this walk,

    my parents and Chela, experiences of life.

CONTENTS

List of Illustrations	vii
Commendatory prefaces	ix
Preface	xi
Acknowledgements	xiii

INTRODUCTION
The Novel and the Representation of Reality	1
Portraits of the Artist	7

PART I: ILLUSORY REALITY AND THE QUESTION OF IDENTITY
The Echoes of Silence	17
Ambiguity: the Ripe Fruit of Postcolonial Discourse	26
"Cogito ergo sum" in Reverse in the Light of Postcolonial Theory	29
The Postcolonial Discourse Implicit in *Birchwood*	31
The Function of the Comic and the Grotesque in Postcolonial Discourse	48

PART II: SCIENCE AND FICTION
A Dialogic Encounter Between Science and Fiction	53
(In)validating *Phenomena* and Fiction	61
The Convenient Form	75
A Synthesis Emanating from Form	81
The Revelation of Fictional Truth	95
Order out of Chaos	107
The "Turning Point" in Literature	124

PART III: THE ART OF WRITING AND THE VISUAL ARTS
The Labyrinth of Multiplicity	127
A Crossroads of Discourses	148

CLOSING REFLECTIONS:
Mirrors and Holographic Labyrinths	157

Bibliography 163

Index 179

LIST OF ILLUSTRATIONS

Fig. 1. A Ptolemaic Map of the World by Andreas Cellarius, *Atlas Coelestis seu Harmonia Macrocosmica* (Amsterdam, 1660). 52

Fig. 2. The Copernican System by Andreas Cellarius, in: *Atlas Coelestis seu Harmonia Macrocosmica* (Amsterdam, 1660). 60

Fig. 3. Kepler's cosmic chalice 82

Fig. 4. Map of the Universe According to Tycho Brahe's System by Andreas Cellarius, in: *Atlas Coelestis seu Harmonia Macrocosmica* (Amsterdam, 1660). 88

Fig. 5. M.C. Escher, "Order and Chaos" (*lithograph, 1950)* 108.

Fig. 6. Jan Vermeer of Delft, "Portrait of a Woman". Museum of Fine arts, Buda-Pesth 126

Fig. 7. Antoine Watteau, "Gilles". Musée du Louvre. 138

COMMENDATORY PREFACE

In this book *Mirrors and Holographic Labyrinths: The Process of a "New" Aesthetic Synthesis in John Banville's Work,* Laura Izarra takes the contemporary Irish writer John Banville to task on the search, recurringly present in his work, for a *new synthesis* in contemporary art and culture, expressed by his stretching to breaking point of the disciplinary limits of art and science, of representation and reality; in short, a questioning of the established frontiers between the reading and the writing of the (known and unknown, past and present) world.

In her analysis of all of Banville's novels published through 1995, Izarra emphasizes the metaphor of the hologram as the basis of Banville's writing, and uses the same metaphor as the basis of her own reading of Banville's work.

In a hologram two or more beams of light are projected onto an object and reflected by multiple mirrors. At the point where the beams intersect a tridimensional image appears and presents to the observer an object metonymically and paradoxically present merely in its absence.

As an Irish Studies scholar and literary critic, the beams of light that Izarra brings to bear on Banville's work include postmodern theory, postcolonial theory, contemporary post-newtonian scientific theories and theories of Discourse, Art, Psychology and History.

From her specific historical and geographic location as a South American, Izarra also projects in her hologram the beams of the writings of noted South American thinkers such as the Argentinian Jorge Luis Borges and the Brazilian Alfredo Bosi.

Contrary to the doomsayers of postmodernism who see the victory of chaos over order, and parallel to Banville's own search for a vision of order in chaos - albeit an immaterial, unpalpable order - Izarra's reading seeks and beholds, amidst the apparent chaos of her multiple theoretical sources, a vision of Banville's vision, and like his, a *new synthesis* which, like the hologram, envisions the paradoxical simultaneity of truth and fiction, art and science, literature and criticism, closure and infinity, presence and absence.

In short, in this book Laura Izarra presents her readers with a truly contemporary banvillean reading of Banville himself.

Lynn Mario T. Menezes de Souza

PREFACE

> One must understand that Art
> is an open act of knowledge,
> it is the boundless fields
> of research work,
> it teaches those
> who face the future.
>
> V.M.

This book is a translation of my doctoral thesis, which was written in Portuguese and submitted at the University of São Paulo, Brazil, in December 1995. For that reason Banville's most recent book, *The Untouchable*, published in 1997, is not mentioned here.

My aim is to define the "new synthesis" proposed by Banville, who foresees the end of postmodernism and the beginning of a new "ism" or synthesis in art. My point of departure is the writer's own *Weltanschauung*, which recognises no frontiers between fiction and reality since the latter is itself a construction of our minds. Banville has said that *"truth is arbitrary, reality is multifarious, language is not a clear lens"*. My analysis of his first nine novels in this book takes the form of an open dialogue with other fields of knowledge, with the critics of his work and contemporary criticism, always based upon the writer's own reflections upon different systems of representation, such as metafiction, science, history, psychoanalysis and the visual arts. My focus is on the interactive process between the observer and the observed in the construction of meanings. The belief that

Literature is a social practice and that literary texts must therefore be analysed within their contexts permeates this work. It has thus been my intention to reveal the effect of the interaction between the writer, the reader and the text within the context of the innumerable reflections, mirror images and possible paths in Banville's labyrinth of narratives. As a South American reader of Irish texts, I firmly believe that Banville's aesthetic synthesis opens up new alternatives of representation which, while not revealing the essence of things, seeks to transform their perception in the form of aesthetic discourse.

In writing my thesis I was very much indebted to the pioneering studies published in the *Irish University Review* Special Issue on Banville edited by Maurice Harmon in 1981 and to the subsequent books by Rüdiger Imhof (1989) and Joseph McMinn (1991). But many of the ideas presented here were developed in a wider conversational network.

My special thanks are due to my supervisor, Dr. Munira Hamud Mutran, whose openness and careful advice gave birth and final shape to my doctoral thesis.

My ideas also owe much to readings, lectures and fortunate encounters with many specialists in the field of Irish Studies: Professor Maurice Harmon from University College Dublin, who introduced me to Banville's work and has constantly provided material for my research; Professor Terence Brown from Trinity College Dublin, where I consulted Banville's manuscripts; Dr. Declan Kiberd for the discussions on Banville's tetralogy when he was a visiting lecturer at the University of São Paulo; Professor Rüdiger Imhof from Wuppertal University (Germany) for the challenging suggestions which guided me throughout my work; Dr. Maureen Murphy from Hofstra University (USA), whose friendly interest has enabled me to keep my bibliography up to date; Dr. Francis Barker and Dr. Peter Hulme for the possibility of a week's research at the University of Essex; my teachers from the University of São Paulo, now my colleagues, and those from the ABRAPUI's Annual Conferences, for their friendship and lively exchange of ideas; my former colleagues and students from

Mackenzie University, Faculdade Ibero-Americana and São Marcos University for their shared knowledge; Dr. Vera Mascarenhas de Campos for giving Portuguese words to my ideas; Peter Harris for the revision of this translation; and, above all, I must thank my distant family for their interest, understanding and encouragement over the past years.

My most profound thanks must also go to John Banville himself, for his kindness and simplicity and for allowing me to interview him in April 1992, in Dublin, where he shared the ideas I have sought to analyse here.

I am also grateful to CAPES for awarding me a scholarship to write this work, and to the British Council and USIS for their financial help towards my participation in International Conferences and visits to British and American university libraries where I collected precious material.

> It is arming people with the power to read, which I see as an absolutely fundamental necessity in order for them to make their way in the present world: this is what I think the study of literature can really do.
>
> J. Hillis Miller, in I. Salusinszky, *Criticism in Society*, p. 209

ACKNOWLEDGEMENTS

Author and publisher wish to thank the following who have kindly given permission for use of copyright material.

Mr. John Banville for allowing me to quote from his novels, Professor Rüdiger Imhof from his writings on Banville and Dr. Alfredo Bosi from his book *Reflexões sobre a Arte,* copyright 1986.

Dr. Anthony Roche, current editor of *Irish University Review. A Journal of Irish Studies* for the extracts from *John Banville Special Issue, Vol 11, N° 1,* copyright 1981.

Woulfhound Press, for the extracts from Rüdiger Imhof's *John Banville: A Critical Introduction,* copyright 1989, by Rüdiger Imhof.

Gill & Macmillan for the extracts from Joseph McMinn's *John Banville: A Critical Study,* copyright 1991, by Joseph McMinn.

The Gallery Press, for quotations from *Nightspawn,* copyright 1993, by John Banville.

Panther Books, for quotations from *Doctor Copernicus, Kepler* and *The Newton Letter*, copyright 1976, 1981 and 1982 respectively, by John Banville.

Macmillan, for extracts from *The Book of Evidence, Ghosts* and *Athena,* copyright 1989, 1993 and 1995 respectively, by John Banville.

Paladin, for extracts from *Birchwood* and *Mefisto*, copyright 1973 and 1986 respectively, by John Banville.

Quotations from various writers cited are credited in the notes or text and are gratefully acknowledged.

INTRODUCTION

> This was a revelation to me: that the outside world is as we perceive or imagine it to be. It does not exist independently of our minds. From that day forth, I realised that reality and fiction were betrothed to each other, that even our ideas are creative fictions. I have always believed that metaphysics, religion and literature all have a common source.
>
> *Jorge Luis Borges*[1]

The Novel and the Representation of Reality

In *The Novel Today,* Malcolm Bradbury states that, ever since the eighteenth century, the evolution of the novel has been divided between, on one hand, *"realism, social documentation and interrelation with historical events and movements"* and, on the other hand, *"form, fictionality and reflexive self-imagination".*[2]

In the first twenty years of this century novelists sought to distance themselves from nineteenth-century reality and to evaluate the creative process of writing within a chaotic context. Dostoievsky, Mann, Joyce, Proust, Faulkner, Virginia Woolf, the exponents of Modernism, were to become the literary paradigm for later writers seeking to emerge from the crisis of the novel and looking for a new

---

[1] "Joyce and Borges: Modernism and the Irish Mind" (Richard Kearney and Seamus Heaney in conversation with Jorge Luis Borges). In: R. Kearney, *Transitions*, p. 53.

poetics of fiction and a better understanding of their art. After World War II the realist novel was reborn, consigning the epistemological questions of the *fin de siècle* to oblivion. However, as Bradbury says, when the liberal expectations of the 1950s began to fail in the 1960s, the epistemological interest in form and technique was reborn as writers attempted to push forward the limits of the art of writing as forgery, as a playful game of signifyings occurring in a surreal dimension. Some of these characteristics were also typical of the modernists, and so contemporary writers, trying to survive in the shadow of Joyce, find they must subvert the conventions of the novel in order to question their essentials and to explore their possibilities, trespassing on the points of tension. Contemporary writers are thus forever remaking the form, using various styles in order to convey historical and cultural contexts that are sometimes perceived as surrealistic. Examples of this process may be seen in Iris Murdoch, when she looks for the nature of language in *Under the Net*, in the satiric and parodic narrative of David Lodge in *Small World*, where he destroys the illusion of reality, in Malcolm Bradbury's comic pessimism in *The History Man*, and in the magic realism of Salman Rushdie in *Midnight's Children* or *Satanic Verses* and of Angela Carter in *The Bloody Chamber*.

The postmodern metafictional novel thus incorporates critical perspectives on the process of writing itself and makes its contribution to a polemical cultural debate, as do other fields of knowledge such as psychoanalysis, aesthetics, linguistics, architecture, and the mass media. The 20th century human being is an empirical and transcendental double, using language to mediate between the unknown and self-knowledge, revealing the relationship of the self to its origin by means of fragmented knowledge. The infinite multiplicity caused by such fragmentation creates a postmodern image of the "real" where chaos, discontinuity and a need for order coexist. In *The Poetics of Postmodernism*, Linda Hutcheon argues that a terminology with negative connotations arises from

---

[2]Malcolm Bradbury, *The Novel Today*, p.8.

this conjunction – *"disunity, discontinuity, decentering, disorder, disruption, fragmentation, indeterminacy, chaos."*[3] The resultant void provokes the self to interrogate the perception of reality as a construction of our minds.

It is in this light that one must view the politically divided world of Ireland, a country whose deeply rooted past has become an eternal present. In Ireland the legendary co-exists with the postmodern. Over the past twenty-five years Northern Ireland has attracted the world's attention due to the growth of violence exercised by IRA and Protestant para-militaries alike. The colonial British presence in the north, with its economic and political power eroded by violence, borders on an independent and multifarious Ireland which is member of the European Community. This juxtaposition reveals great religious (Protestant versus Catholic), cultural, economic, social and political (Unionist versus Nationalist) scissions. Fragmentation, decentering, disorder and chaos, products of the political situation of the country and of the time we live in, have been aggravated by the country's culturally and politically divided identity, even after the end of the armed terrorist campaign in 1994. There are Irish people who proudly proclaim themselves to be British whilst nonetheless affirming their "difference" in the North; and in the South there are Irish who are proudly independent and yet use a language that has been appropriated from the "Other". This reveals not only the duality of the Irish mind but also the multiplicity of the postcolonial Anglo-Irish identity.

Irish writers like Yeats, Joyce and Beckett attempted to explain this phenomenon by questioning language itself from a nationalist context, from art *for its own sake* to the absurd, in the process changing the rules of writing and transcending their own geographical limits. Contemporary writers such as Brian Friel, Seamus Heaney, John Banville, Neil Jordan have devoted themselves to the dilemma in a historical context, dealing with the interaction between past and present. They have revisited and re-created reality poetically, using different kinds

---

[3] Linda Hutcheon, *The Poetics of Postmodernism*, p.3

of media. Such writers have become part of a cultural revolution that is generating a new awareness of the meaning of *being Irish*, both in the north and the south of Ireland. With purely intransitive trends from the written word to oral, musical, cinematographic forms, the aesthetic innovation of these writers is an invitation to reflect upon the state of art and knowledge controlled by genre, subjectivization and text from a postmodern and postcolonial plural perspective.

Plurality provokes in the intimacy of the human being an unrest and desire for synthesis, for the fusion of opposites into a new form retaining what is legitimate and offering, as a result, a new and superior point of view. It is precisely because of John Banville's skills of fusion and synthesis that his work stands out in the socio-political and cultural context of Ireland and the postmodern literary context in general. His literary work explores the interrelations between fiction and metafiction, science, psychoanalysis and the visual arts in a constant search for a "new synthesis" that will interact with a multiplicity of meanings.

I do not wish to become embroiled in the debate concerning the nature of postmodernism, but rather to develop new concepts within the indefinite and illusory field of contemporary fiction. I wish to focus upon Banville's novels because, convinced that modernism and postmodernism no longer exist, he offers a "new" proposal for synthesis which embraces the plurality of Ireland's specific literary and historical context:

> We are on the threshold of a new **ism**, a new synthesis. What will it be? I do not know. But I hope it will be an art which is honest enough to despair and yet go on; rigorous and controlled, cool and yet passionate, without delusions, aware of its own possibilities and its own limits; an art which knows that truth is arbitrary, that reality is multifarious, that language is not a clear lens. Did I say new? What I have defined is as old as Homer.[4]

Banville's "manifesto" has provided me with a kind of Ariadne's thread in the labyrinth of my research, since Banville "defines" the "new synthesis" in an indefinite and multiple way where the past is a referent in the transition towards

---
[4] John Banville, "A Talk". In: *IUR*. Vol. 11, No.1, p.17

the unknown. This apparent contradiction provided the starting point for a discussion of the way in which he re-creates *signifieds* and articulates *differences*, proposing a new means of representation in the field of fiction.

Ever since the Middle Ages artists have been seeking correspondences with Nature, with "reality", adopting different theoretical and empirical means in their search. Several syntheses were formulated after the French, Flemish and Italian synthesis of Heaven and Earth in the fifteenth century, using either symbols or scientific methods to reconcile Christian tradition with Neo-Naturalism. In the sixteenth and seventeenth centuries such syntheses appeared within either a religious or a heretical context. Only one, heretical, voice was heard which denied the new concepts of the universe resulting from new scientific formulae which attempted to explain observable natural phenomena. The relationship between world and language was governed by the laws of similitude whereas classical thought concerned itself with the relationship between names and the order of things, questioning the current methods of interpretation and giving priority to the power of discourse. The eighteenth century produced a symmetrical discontinuity, distancing the possibility of synthesis from the space of representation. If, in the past, the ordering principle had been that of successive differences and identities, in the nineteenth century it was analogy and succession that revealed identity through the relationship between various elements and their functions. Realism and scientific naturalism played with the word in the world of representation, while language did not interact with representations, avoiding discursive forms. According to Foucault in *Le mots et les choses*, language self-defined itself in the act of writing at the beginning of modernism. It was then that language entered the field of Philosophy, revealing the genesis of an *enigmatic multiplicity* that was to become visible in postmodernism.

What does Banville mean by a *"new synthesis"* when he admits its multiplicity and, at the same time, tries to explain its essence? Up to what point is it a new aesthetic practice within the postmodern context of the novel? It is not my intention here to offer a final and closed answer to these questions, but rather to outline the poetics which, faced with the impossibility of representing the essence of things, articulate the cultural discourses and processes of various social practices representing different ways of perceiving the world, and transform them into an aesthetic discourse in order to produce a new synthesis. Banville questions the old limits of representation and goes beyond the borders of postmodernism revealing the existence of a new order out of chaos in fiction.

This concept of order out of chaos echoes Prigogine and Stengers's new scientific principle stated in their book *Order Out of Chaos. Man's New Dialogue with Nature*.[5] The authors explain that order and chaos no longer co-exist and have, instead, formed a new synthesis: nonequilibrium, the flow of matter and energy, may be a source of order. If our contemporary concern is with the paradox of order being created out of chaos, they believe that humanity is heading towards a "new synthesis", a new concept of nature ("new naturalism") that has as its symbol the most beautiful manifestations of sculpture: *"the search for a junction between stillness and motion, time arrested and time passing."* [6]

Aware of the evolution of knowledge and the influence of science and technology on the human mind, Banville perambulates at the margins of the novel, interrogating the constructions of realities. He deconstructs different world views in the fields of fiction, science, psychology, history and painting, opening the way for a new poetic synthesis of stillness and motion, arbitrary truth and multifaceted reality, where language is *"a nebulous lens"* whose aesthetic value is to project the multiplicity of the unit.

---

[5] Ilya Prigogine won the 1977 Nobel Prize for Chemistry for his work on the thermodynamics of nonequilibrium systems. The book mentioned here is the departure point to understand Banville's "new synthesis" and other readings of scientific revolutions that have been fictionalised by the Irish writer.

[6] Ilya Prigogine & Isabelle Stengers, *Order Out of Chaos. Man's new dialogue with nature.* p.22.

Portraits of the Artist

My intention here is to present sketches of portraits of the artist and his work painted by other scholars. These sketches will provide the background against which my own swirling brushstrokes will, I hope, give new light and shade to the writer's figure as I seek to paint new pictures of his art in the course of this study.

John Banville was born in Wexford 1945 and published his first book, *Long Lankin*, in 1970. After fourteen years he authorised the publication of a second edition of the book, with some changes that reveal the excellence of style of a mature writer. The *leitmotiv* of this series of nine stories and a novella was an old Scottish ballad that provides the symbolic structure for various modern psychological fictions. Though the book shows the writer at his experimental stage, this study will focus on his nine subsequent novels because, in his search for the essence of a work of art, Banville develops a project modelled on different scientific systems which reveal to him a "form" and a "new synthesis" in fiction.

His first two novels, *Nightspawn* (1971) and *Birchwood* (1973), are deconstructions of the limits of metafiction. The tetralogy idealised by the writer[7]- *Doctor Copernicus* (1976), *Kepler* (1981), *The Newton Letter* (1982) and *Mefisto* (1986), focuses on the biographies of the scientists Copernicus, Kepler, Newton and Einstein, to analyse their creative processes and compare them with those of artists. Painting provides the model for the trilogy, *The Book of Evidence* (1989), *Ghosts* (1993) and *Athena* (1995), where he immerses himself in the fragmented human psyche and wanders through the labyrinth of the human mind.

Banville's success abroad started in 1989 when his novel *The Book of Evidence*, was shortlisted for the Booker Prize, the major prize in English Literature. Although the winner that year was Kazuo Ishiguro with *Remains of the Day*, Banville received the Guinness Peat Aviation Award for the novel, which was

---
[7] Rüdiger Imhof, "An Interview with John Banville". In: *IUR*, Vol. 11, No.1, 1981. P. 12

added to his previous prizes: the American-Irish Foundation Literary Award, a Macauley Fellowship, the Allied Irish Banks Prize, and the James Tait Black Memorial Prize, in 1976, for *Doctor Copernicus,* and the Guardian Fiction Prize, in 1981, for *Kepler*. His work has been the subject of study by some important scholars such as Rüdiger Imhof, who wrote a pioneering essay, published in a Special Issue of *The Irish University Review on Banville* edited by Maurice Harmon in 1981. In "John Banville's Supreme Fiction",[8] he analyses *Kepler* as a supreme work of fiction due to the book's exaltation of form in the art of writing. Imhof subsequently published the formalist *John Banville: A Critical Introduction,* in which he highlights the self-referentiality and intertextuality of the writer's work. In a recent unpublished essay, "In Search of the Rosy Grail: The Creative Process in the Novels of John Banville"[9], Imhof synthesises his previous ideas and analyses how Banville mixes various genres and narrative conventions, mentioning very briefly the relation between art and reality and the theory of improbability and uncertainty.

In 1988, Joseph McMinn also wrote an essay "Stereotypical Images of Ireland in John Banville's Fiction",[10] which was the seed for the full-length book *John Banville. A Critical Study*. McMinn concentrates on the poetic character of fiction and develops a theme rejected by Imhof: the question of realism in Banville's fiction. His thesis is based on the self-reflective narrative that Banville learned from Joyce, Beckett and Flann O'Brien, which, despite being distanced from realism through symbolism and parody, *"offers Banville the kind of imaginative freedom that allows him both to imitate and exploit the Irish tradition".*[11] McMinn believes that the writer tries to represent the *"mystery of reality",* so he analyses in particular detail the presence of such Irish stereotypes as the lost language, "the Big House" and the landscape in Banville's writing.

---

[8] In: *IUR*. Vol.11, No.1, 1981. pp.52-86.
[9] Professor Imhof sent me a copy of this essay (probably unpublished) after I met him at Wuppertal University in May 1993.
[10] Joseph McMinn, In: *Eire-Ireland*, 23,3. Fall 1988. pp.94-102
[11] Joseph McMinn, *John Banville. A Critical Study*, p.9

However, Banville rejects the notion of the novel as a mirror of reality. Francis Molloy confirms this in "The Search for Truth: The Fiction of John Banville", another pioneering essay, referring to an interview of 15th April 1976, *"Indeed, he has always been more interested in form than content and has never believed that fiction should deal with social, domestic or political affairs"*.[12]

Using Robert Scholes's terminology, Molloy says that Banville's narratives are *fabulations* because they move from realistic to artistic fiction. In another essay, Patrick O'Neill's derridean approach reveals the gap between the real (which in his words is *no more than a convenient fiction*[13]) and any attempt to grasp it (which could only be a fiction), focusing on Banville's fictional characteristics of difference and discontinuity. Banville rejects mimetic realism, practising it in a subversive way which calls conventional concepts of reality into question. He is a parodic writer who questions reality rather than imitating it. He uses Irish stereotypes to challenge the traditional narrative *clichés* and he relates the obsession of modernism, the crisis of imagination, to the facts of a historical world. Seamus Deane discussed this concept before O"Neill in 'Be Assured I am Inventing': The fiction of John Banville"[14] and he also argues polemically that everything that Banville wrote up to 1975 was *"a prolegomena to a fiction rather than a fiction itself."* He adds that Banville cannot write a novel until he sees what one is and that he cannot see what one is until he writes one.[15]

Imhof was the first to attack this radical vision of Banville as a *"litterateur who has a horror of producing 'literature'"* and who *"joyfully commits technical narcissism"*.[16] However, in the unrecorded interview I had with Banville in April 1992 he agreed with Seamus Deane's criticism and said that he was still trying to discover how to write a novel. Although the novel is a relatively new genre it began to decay after Joyce and Beckett. Banville believes that the mass media

---

[12]Francis C. Molloy, In: *IUR*, Vol. 11, No.1, 1981. p.30.
[13]Patrick O'Neill, "John Banville". In *SECL Studies in English and Comparative Literature*. p. 207.
[14]In: Patrick Rafroidi & Maurice Harmon, (eds.) *The Irish Novel in Our Time*. pp.329-338.
[15]*Ibid.*, 332.

have doomed the novel to extinction and it will only survive in universities. The collective mind knows something which is failing and fiction is losing its popularity.[17] He says, *"We are as in the 1890's, a period of Dark Ages. It is the end of the novel, but something new will take place"* (Interview, 1992).

Banville also revealed, in a previous interview with Professor Imhof, that, even though he failed in *Nightspawn*, the most important point is the *"quality of that failure"*[18]:

> I don't mean this in the way that Graham Greene, let us say, would mean it. I am speaking not of the lost battle of life, but of something entirely other, that is, art-as-failure. Do I make myself obscure?[19]

In *Transitions: Narratives in Modern Irish Culture*, Richard Kearney argues that few writers decide to question the possibilities of writing. He calls this critical trend in fiction a *"counter-tradition"* and he analyses Banville's first novels as examples of that transition from a medieval comprehension of reality to a modern one that questions the (im)possibility of writing about it[20]. Imhof echoes this statement, showing that Banville is writing critical fiction to *"find a cure for art"*.[21]

The first three books of the tetralogy about the scientists attracted the attention of the Canadian critic Linda Hutcheon from the point of view of the theory of the novel and, in her book *The Poetics of Postmodernism*, she analyses them as *historiographic metafictions*. She argues that the limits between biography and novel disappear, despite the existence of a problematic fusion of the conventions of the two genres.[22]

A metafiction is a fictional narrative that highlights its own artificial status in questioning the relationship between fiction and reality. Banville centres all his

---

[16] Rüdiger Imhof, *John Banville. A Critical Introduction*. p.9.
[17] Ronan Sheehan, "Novelists on the Novel". In: *The Crane Bag*, III, 1, 1979. pp.79-80.
[18] *IUR*. Vol.11, No.1, 1981. p.5.
[19] *Ibid.*, p.5
[20] Richard Kearney, *Transitions: Narratives in Modern Irish Culture* p.93
[21] Rüdiger Imhof, *John Banville. A Critical Introduction*. p.10.
[22] Linda Hutcheon. *Op. Cit.*, p.113.

aesthetic energy on constructions of reality, and he believes that, in order to achieve an aesthetic "density", a quality in art, the things said should be subordinated to the way they are said. Therefore, for Banville, the only way is form – *"In art the only absolute criterion is shape, form, ratio, harmony, call it what you will, call it order".*[23]

This order that Banville advocates is not sequential or linear. Imhof believes it is a *"spatial"* one, *"a kind of order relying on multiple planes of relationships".*[24] The concept of order within chaos is the central theme of this thesis, as I believe it is associated with Banville's conviction concerning the existence of a new synthesis in the field of fiction and also with other fields of knowledge, as well as with social changes, disorder, instability, diversity and disequilibrium, characteristics of the contemporary world. According to him, science has changed our notion of the world while psychoanalysis has changed our view of human beings and it seems to him that *"artists haven't caught up with that all."*[25]

The concept of (im)possibility of a synthesis incorporating multiplicity has not yet been subjected to critical analysis. Postmodernism appears to deny any kind of synthesis related to the plurality of meanings *per se*. Banville succeeds in exploring the limits of representation and recreates an order out of chaos in fiction, moving freely between the various fields of knowledge, taking different systems as critical models and translating their theoretical principles for use in the realm of writing.

In order to demonstrate Banville's "new aesthetic synthesis" I have divided this work into three parts, corresponding to the three systems with which the writer enters into dialogue in his critical evaluation of what fiction is.

In the first part, *Nightspawn* and *Birchwood* are analysed. In these novels Banville deconstructs metafiction, questioning its very essence. There is a rupture of the delimitation between fiction and its criticism, provoking a tension in the

---

[23] John Banville. "Physics and Fiction: Order from Chaos". In: *The New York Book Review*, 21 April 1985. p.41.
[24] Rüdiger Imhof, *John Banville. A Critical Introduction.* p.17.

two fields at the point of their possible fusion. His writing raises doubts concerning the self-referential limits of metafictional discourse through the reconstruction of an "artifact" representing reality composed of syntheses of fossilised forms such as the detective novel and the autobiography. Banville uses different discourses in his attempt to represent the essence of reality as he seeks to create a new literary identity within an Irish historical context.

The second part focuses on Banville's exploration of new methods and his diachronic questioning of other syntheses, in particular those scientific syntheses which resulted in new conceptions of the universe and established new meanings in the field of knowledge. The writer explores the realm of physics in order to reactivate traditionally incompatible themes - literature and science - and to establish co-relations between the formation of concepts, chains of enunciations and discursive formations. Thus, he argues against the illusory antagonism which sees scientific and literary narratives as opposite discursive practices: objective-descriptive versus subjective-poetic respectively. The analysis of the tetralogy shows how Banville dissects the processes of the scientists' discoveries in order to understand the mind-set that guided their experiments. In the metafictional field, the discoveries are seen as constructions of the scientists' minds because they were seeking to explain theories which they had created *a priori* concerning sensorily perceived observations. Scientific "truth" is questioned through metaphorical discourse in *Doctor Copernicus* and *Kepler*. This probable and predictable "truth" conflicts with the social context in *The Newton Letter*, and is then relativized in *Mefisto*, where the scientist has to rely on his own intuition, as Kepler once affirmed.

In the final part, the analysis of the trilogy demonstrates how fiction is in fact an illusory process of representation of reality in the search for a monological synthesis if it is considered that *"truth is arbitrary, that reality is multifarious, that language is not a clear lens"*. *The Book of Evidence*, *Ghosts* and *Athena* each

---

[25] Ronan Sheehan, "Novelists on the Novel". In: *The Crane Bag*, III, 1, 1979. pp.79-80.

have painting as a model and all three books question the limits of reference, representation and significance, territories traditionally claimed by poetry and painting. My critical perspective focuses on the interaction between the observer and the object observed – whether this be between the narrator and the work of art, or the narrator and social practices, or the narrator and his own psyche – and is based on Banville's concept of the theory of reception. Influenced by Wallace Stevens, the writer describes how the mind retains an experience and how the imagination processes its own constructions of that experience. Memory is therefore seen to be essential for the imagination to be able to produce the non-familiar using the familiar.

Finally, I shall leave the reader with some open questions concerning the "new synthesis" proposed by Banville. Is it similar to what Walter Benjamin calls "synthetic forms" of experience and narrative, a constructivist contrasting of the privacy of individual experience in contemporary capitalist society against the spontaneous experience and narrative of a traditional society, resulting from the decadence of the communal memory and tradition that guaranteed shared collective experience? Is it this concept that generates "minimalism" in art?[26]

Or is Banville's "new synthesis" more akin to Iris Murdoch's image of dryness when she refers to the pure, clean and self-contained symbol?[27] Is Banville referring to a contradictory postmodern art that validates the ideas of plurality within chaos and disorder within order and, in so doing, demystifies our attempts to structure chaos in order to give a meaning to our lives?... Or should it better be seen as an echo of the Newtonian synthesis which expressed a systematic alliance between the theoretical comprehension of nature and the practical manipulation of it?[28] Or is this "new synthesis" similar to the "objective syntheses" outlined by Michael Foucault when he analyses the limits of representation? In this case, is it an *a priori* synthesis in which the transcendental subject identifies a possible

---

[26]Walter Benjamin, *Obras escolhidas*. p.10.
[27]Iris Murdoch, "Against Dryness. A Polemical Sketch". In Bradbury, M. *The Novel Today*. p.28.
[28]Ilya Prigogine & Isabelle Stengers. *Order Out of Chaos*. p.39.

synthesis among the various representations, or is it an *a posteriori* synthesis where the essences cannot be identified except by their laws?[29] Or, finally, can Banville's synthesis be represented best in terms of the heterotopias that Foucault identified in Borges's narratives which explore the boundaries between differences and similarities?

Due to the different systems used by Banville as models and his extensive knowledge of critical theories and fiction, and the exhaustive research he carried out in the fields of history, science, psychoanalysis and painting in order to write his books, I have adopted the methodology of comparative literature in my analysis. I have also employed a deconstructive reading technique in order to establish a simultaneous dialogue both with the writer and with the contemporary critical, scientific and philosophical conceptualisations that provide the background to his creative process and enable the reader to elucidate Banville's theoretical principles and beliefs concerning the theory of the novel.

Some modern and postmodern writers like Banville ignore the limits between fiction and science. For example, Borges claims that scientific discourse itself is a fictional form of expression. To be able to construct challenging literature, Borges believes that writers and critics alike should explore the field of science and seek to understand how scientific discourse conveys a general comprehension of natural phenomena. Physics and Mathematics, History, Psychology and Fine Arts each offer knowledge that enriches readers who do not need to be specialists in order to be thus enlightened. In his novels, Banville himself makes ironic reference to some concepts related to scientific "truths" which were subsequently proved to be untrue or entirely opposite to the truth. Emboldened by Banville's own example, then, I have ventured down the roads of science in my quest as a researcher into fictions.

Thus, in the course of this thesis, I shall attempt to sketch out Banville's synthesis. Some of the shading in this sketch will be stronger than others as I draw

---

[29]Michel Foucault, les mots et les choses . Trans. a*s palavras e as coisas. Uma arqueologia das*

upon tones drawn from postcolonial theory, postmodernism, Science, Philosophy, Art, History, Psychology and literary criticism, in order to communicate new interpretations of the author's art, always referring back to Banville's theoretical convictions expressed explicitly in various interviews, reviews or articles, or implicitly in his novels. At the end of the thesis I draw attention to the fact that, apart from a few reviews, there is very little critical writing concerning the writer's work.

Critical readers will construct their own understanding of Banville's aesthetic synthesis from the threads of my discursive net and will, I hope, interact with the questions I raise in order to produce their own interpretative order. The dialogue with other critics throughout my analysis of Banville's work, together with the reader's own critical interaction will give the different shades to the portrait I propose to paint in the following pages.

I

ILLUSORY REALITY

AND THE QUESTION OF IDENTITY

> . . . .
> Mac Morris, gallivanting
> round the Globe, whinged
> to courtier and groundling
> who had heard tell us
>
> as going very bare
> of learning, as wild hares,
> as anatomies of death:
> 'What ish my nation?'
>
> And sensibly, though so much
> later, the wandering Bloom
> replied, 'Ireland,' said Bloom,
> 'I was born here. Ireland.'
> Seamus Heaney, "Traditions"

The Echoes of Silence

If modernism was obsessed with "the crisis of imagination" and its relationship with the facts of the historical world, the postmodern debate has focused on "the crisis of representation" and the illusion of realism. This relationship between fiction and reality is questioned by metafiction, which reveals, through the self-conscious use of language, an uncertainty about the validity of representations.

In Banville's first novels, metafiction is inextricably intertwined with the elements of the writer's postcolonial consciousness, inserted in a post-Joycean literary context. Banville's fight for self-definition in the art of writing, for a literary identity, impels him to construct a theory of fiction that, according to him, goes beyond postmodernism.

Believing that the very nature of fiction is artificial, the writer deconstructs the elements of metafiction in *Nightspawn* (1971) and *Birchwood* (1973), and again in the third book of the tetralogy - *The Newton Letter*, in search of a "new aesthetic synthesis". He reveals that colonial stereotypes and postcolonial assumptions exist in a state of subliminal tension within the chaos of narrative. In order to understand the past and find a new way of writing fiction, he draws freely upon the fields of metafiction and critical theory, moving parodically from the romantic ideal of nationalist discourse to the chaos of postmodern discourse in an attempt to represent reality and prove the existence of order within chaos.

His first novel, *Nightspawn* (1971), is about a writer writing an autobiographic novel focused upon a particular socio-political moment in his life in a foreign land, which finishes with his initiation as a writer and artist, an echo of Stephen's epiphany in *A Portrait of the Artist as a Young Man*:

> It was a perfect evening . . . Shadows gathered. I watched the night approach over a far hill, and suddenly I was assailed by a sense of continuity, of unity, of things following one on the other. I cannot explain, I have not the energy. . . . Whatever I did, or might do, the world went on, with or without me, always, and I was but a small part of an eternal confluence which I could not understand. I am talking about the healing of wounds. I am talking about art. (*N.*, p.198-99)[1]

In *John Banville: A Critical Study*, Joseph McMinn detects part of the process, explaining how the main character, Ben White, insists upon reinventing a past that cannot be reproduced. In *John Banville. A Critical Introduction*, Imhof had previously pointed out the metafictionality of the novel, saying that Banville's aim was to write about the art of writing using a self-reflective narrative discourse. Imhof also analysed how Banville created a novel of suspense based on the traditional *thriller*, and affirmed that the writer's metafictional intention occurs at two levels: the story itself and the writer's intrusions into it.

However, neither Imhof nor McMinn referred to the subtle presence of an incipient postcolonial novel, which was to become more manifest in *Birchwood* and *The Newton Letter*. The fictional autobiographical narrative is self-engendered as the narrator selects facts from the past. It has the double aim of discovering both its own identity and also what had been lost due to the political aspect of the facts, establishing an element of complicity with the reader. The narrator not only reveals the facts as he knew them but also his philosophy of life when he questions the limits between past and present, between the task of writing about his own life and life itself, between the political and socio-historical context and its denial.

Nightspawn is set during the military regime in Greece from 1924 to 1928. According to Imhof, the narrator is bound by the narrative conventions of the detective novel genre. I myself believe that, although there are indeed many coincidences, intrigues and conspiracies, these are subject to a reverse movement as crossroads become *cul-de-sacs* or circular labyrinths where Ben White's inquisitorial questions concerning the formulated plan are greeted with silence. He seems not to know what is happening around him even though he is an important piece in the game of revolutionary intrigue. According to Banville, the reader who looks for clues in order to solve the conundrum, as in a traditional detective novel, will be deceived because art is fraudulent.

> A lie is only a lie when the one lied to thinks he is hearing the truth. When the lier and the listener both know it is a lie, then the lie becomes transformed into ritual. Henry James recognised this, which makes him for me the first modern novelist. Society, he tells us, lives by, can only live by, necessary falsehoods. Art is one of them - the Supreme Fiction, as Wallace Stevens calls it.[2]

---

[1] Quotations refer to the following edition: Banville, J. *Nightspawn*. County Meath:The Gallery Press,1993.
[2] John Banville, "A Talk". In: *IUR*, Vol.11, No. 1, Spring 1981, p.16

Banville said that he chose a political theme precisely *"to make nothing of it"*, just as a shadow disappears when the sun sets. The novel thus becomes a metaphor for the futility of attempting to comprehend reality through fiction.

> When I came to write my first novel, *Nightspawn,* the attitude which I adopted was one of extreme distrust of the novel form itself. I set out to subject the traditional, nineteenth-century concept to as much pressure as I could bring to bear on it, while yet remaining within the rules. I made a wildly implausible plot. I chose stock characters. I brought in a political theme - the Colonels' coup in Greece - precisely in order to make nothing of it. There were many reasons for proceeding in this way, but one of the principal ones was that I was interested to test, to bend close to breaking, the very curious relationship which exists between a reader and his author. I wished to challenge the reader to go on suspending his disbelief in my fiction in the face of an emphatic admission on my part that what I was presenting was fiction and nothing more - and everything more.[3]

Imhof identifies and analyses the elements typical of *thrillers* and gangster films used by the author, for example, the wild chase of the hero after his opponent, the love story in the middle of the espionage, confession scenes that explain why the villains acted as they did, as well as the story's climax. The analogy between the novel and the detective story is rendered explicit by the ironic narrative of the fictional writer as he reminds the reader of the artifices he is using in his constant pseudo-authorial interventions, and also by Banville's own interventions in the fictional narrative.

However, I believe that Banville is actually using the kind of discourse that the postcolonial critic Homi Bhabha describes as *"articulated silences",*[4] which mark particular absences twisting the various significances of the text and dislocating the "contradictions". Silence therefore fulfils a subversive role in Banville's narrative. For Banville, writing is *"a struggle with the insidious whisper of*

---

[3]Rüdiger Imhof, "An Interview with John Banville". In: *IUR*, op.cit., p.5
[4]Homi Bhabha, "Signs Taken for Wonders: Questions of Ambivalence and Authority under a Tree Outside Delhi, May 1817". In: *Critical Inquiry* 12, Autumn 1985. pp.144-165.
& Lynn Mário Menezes de Souza, in his doctoral thesis *"O Rato que Ruge: O discurso crítico-literário pós-colonial como suplemento",* pp.30-31 when he refers to repression in colonial literature (an ideological closure).

silence", synonymous not with failure but with honesty, as he once stated in a letter to his American publisher W.W. Norton & Company:

> One has to build up a base which is nearest to the honesty of silence, and begin from there. *Nightspawn*, for me, is as near to silence as I can get, at the moment.[5]

This honesty has an aesthetic and political value and hides the absence of plenitude. In this absence/silence, opposites are no longer in a state of confrontation and generate new meanings which are articulated as supplements to the original when it is dislocated and which open a space for the Derridean differences present in the questionings. The reader must use appropiate strategies in order to break this silence and transform it into a deleted voice.

For example, in *Nightspawn*, the theme contains an intrinsic ambiguity, producing a play on words which results in a combination of different significances equating to the universal theme of the *thriller* ("the original"), where traditionally the narrator has complete power over the narrative. The narrator of *Nightspawn* shows this in the last part of the book when he says he is revealing his theme:

> Before I move at last into the real grit and gristle of things, I have a little riddle. Perceive. One word, three syllables. The first is a wager. The second is a fish. The third is one third less than everything, and the whole is my theme. What is it? (*N.*, p.143)

"Betrayal!" It is not only a betrayal of the detective story as a form but also a betrayal of the reader by the author. This displacement leads the reader to completely disbelieve what the author is narrating because the latter admits that he is only presenting fiction. The third dimension is the novelist's betrayal of himself, when he reveals his secrets and stratagems for dealing with the art of writing:

---

[5]Rüdiger Imhoff, *John Banville. A Critical Introduction*. pp. 38-39.

> *Nightspawn* is a kind of betrayal, of the reader's faith in the writer's good faith, and also it is a betrayal of, if you like, the novelist's guild and its secret signs and stratagems. It is an inside-out novel, it wears its skeleton and its nerves on the outside.[6]

But this process of revelation carries an extra-textual power, its own context, which discloses through silences exactly what the writer does not reveal consciously. Silence as a supplement to the original has the subversive function of questioning the writer's unconscious.

Banville uses a similar technique to that employed by Velázquez in his masterpiece *Las Meninas* (*The Maids of Honour*). He portrays a novelist engaged in the production of an autobiographical novel, being observed in the process of doing so. He freezes and dissects this image, showing it to the reader in order that he/she may observe how the writer-author performs the act of creation. However, Banville simultaneously subverts the image of *mise en abîme* with the concomitant, paradoxical processes of a centralising analysis focused upon the origin of the image and a decentralising one which opens the narrative up to external and extra-textual consequences, - centripetal and centrifugal vortices to use Bakhtin's terminology.[7]

The *mise en abîme* also produces an effect which I have described as "an aesthetic food chain", metaphorically suggested by chain reactions at various points in the narrative:

> I looked at the pelican. The pelican looked at the dog. The dog barked suddenly, and the old man, with a terrible roar, gave it a clout of his stick and sent the miserable animal howling across the quay. The barber awoke,... (*N.*, p.13)

These techniques of *mise en abîme* and of "an aesthetic food chain" result in the movement of *supplementarity* made possible by the lack or absence of a centre or

---

[6]Rüdiger Imhof, "An Interview with John Banville". In: *IUR*, Vol.11, No.1, p. 6.
[7]Michael Bakhtin, *The Dialogic Imagination*. Trans. U.S.A.: University of Texas Press, 1981

origin which was identified by Derrida.[8] This game of substitutions occurs when the sign inscribes itself in the centre as a surplus, as a supplement, in addition to the lack on the part of the signified which reveals its own lack of totalization. This process is analogous to Banville's endless look and aesthetic chain because there is a similar destabilisation of the signified when reviewed in the dynamic movement of the sign in relation to its antecedent and to the extra-textual elements. The narrator explains the act of remembering as follows:

> ... that day I thought about the island, and now I think about thinking about the island, and tomorrow, tomorrow I shall think about thinking about thinking about the island, and all will be one, however I try, and there will be no separate thoughts, but only one thought, one memory, and I shall still know nothing.(*N.*, p.102)

The new thought generated by the previous ones will become a single memory, different from its antecedents but which will nonetheless not reveal itself as a totalization, as the authentic truth; it will be a questioned truth, a *supplement* of the origin, adding a movement of signification to the signifieds.

Memory plays a significant role in postcolonial discourse when it acts at the limits of uncertainty. In *Culture and Imperialism*, Edward Said argues that recalling the past is one of the most commonly used strategies in interpreting the present but what makes the strategy polemical is the uncertainty about whether the past is already finished, or whether it still continues in different forms. This gives origin to debates on influence, true or false judgement, present facts and future priorities.[9] In *Nightspawn*, Banville focuses on the fallibility of the narrator, which is directly relationed to the uncertainty mentioned above.

The narrator invokes Memory (*"Mnemosyne, that lying whore"*), because the narrated facts are not so evident as they were presented as being, and he denounces the arbitrary power of selection:

---

[8] Jacques Derrida, J. "Structure , Sign and Play in the Discourse of Human Sciences". In: Lodge, D. *Modern Criticism and Theory*. London: Longman, 1988. p.119.
[9] Edward Said, *Culture and Imperialism*, p.1

> The process of artistic selection sometimes eliminates the nuances which mislead. I have tried to retain a few of them, but they have a fishy smell. Anyway, I think that it should be... look, what am I excusing? What do I care? I am the boss around here, of course I am, and I shall do as I like, so put that in your column and criticise it. (*N.*, p.157).

There are unsuccessful attempts to give order to chaos after the reversal of the discourse in which the omniscient and authoritarian narrator is seen to be incapable of historicism, of writing facts in a linear way based on causality. Nothing can be affirmed as being true, everything is a metaphor.

Thus, in his very first novel, Banville questions, by means of a fictional pseudo-autobiographical narrative, the narrated "truth", the fictitious order of the textual and extra-textual facts. This questioning was to reach its climax in his tetralogy on the scientists who changed the conception of the universe, in which the fictional pseudo-autobiographical narrative was substituted by a metafictional one, in the third person, and then in its turn replaced first-person narration, but this time from a wider perspective.

In my opinion, the autobiographical text questions the failure of narrative and establishes a virtual dialogue between the fictional narrator and the reader, a process that resembles Banville's *aesthetic food chain*. The narrator manipulates facts of the past to reveal only what he is interested in and what he recalls of his life. The undisclosed past feeds the drama, provoking a symbiosis between the act of narrating and the drama of the narrative itself. Memory fails and reveals the narrator's fallibility before the uncertainty of the past. Throughout the novel the narrator is constantly casting doubt on his own chronology - *"My chronology is all wrong. No matter* (124). *"Chronology again, all out of whack. Makes not a bit of damn difference now"* (183).

At the same time, the narrator commands the virtual reader to observe the sequence of time to judge its veracity. The novel of memory fails in its ambiguity. The narrated action already belongs to the past and the sequence of facts within the chaotic context of the narrative acquires multiple connotations, creating ambivalent principles. There is a slow overlapping of thin and transparent levels in an attempt to show that, even though chaos exists, there will be no oblivion because *"recollections do not decay, unless I should forget, and I shall not forget. Take these moments. Treat them with care, for they are my inheritance"*(109).

Uncertainty concerning the past generates silent voids which, in their turn, produce louder sounds which create a range of significations when silence is the *supplement* of what should have been said. Banville closes his second novel *Birchwood* emphasising the primacy of silence when he echoes Wittgenstein's statement: *"wherof I cannot speak, thereof I must be silent"* (175).

In both novels, this silence will be only perceived by those who have acute hearing. Derrida, theorising on the autobiography, argues that only the other will be able to close the signified, and he calls the form *otobiography* because it is the ear of the other that will constitute the *"autos"* of the autobiography.[10] The narrator will finish his autobiography when the other has *heard* the *differences* with his acute hearing, understood the meanings and has been seduced by the received message.

The political implications of the *otobiography* within a postcolonial context are evident in the case of those postcolonial cultures that still use the colonizer's language as the official language of the country. The aim is to be heard by the other, to transform the particular into the universal in the search for self-affirmation before the other, in the search for identity. The autobiographical narrative, even a fictional one as in this case, plays this function, resulting in the recognition of the other and of oneself in the other.

---

[10] Jacques Derrida, *The Ear of the Other*, p. 51

Ambiguity: The Ripe Fruit of Postcolonial Discourse

To conclude my analysis of *Nightspawn* I shall now turn to the ways in which the various meanings of the title of the novel overlap and acts as supplements in the process of signification. The literal meaning of the title is "eggs – or offspring - of the night" and it has a bipolar political connotation: a positive one because it refers to engendered life, and a negative one because it belongs to the night, to darkness. These opposite meanings are articulated by the writer and reveal the stereotype of the colonised, fruit of colonial discourse: "born to be a troublemaker".[11] Thus, it carries negative political and psychological connotations due to the historical determinism of colonial Ireland. Ben White discloses his origin when he claims that rituals frighten him:

> Everything frightens me. The sea, the sky. I suffer from not only claustrophobia but also agoraphobia. I was born in the darkest hour of the darkest night in a black year, and -(*N.*, p.40)

This metaphorical image of the spawn of Satan relates directly to the opening paragraph of the novel which, according to Imhof, is an example of intertextuality, referring as it does to Dostoievsky's *Notes from Underground – "I am a sick man, I am a spitful man. I think my life is diseased. Only a flood of spleen now could cauterise my wounds"* (11).

The power of the other to underestimate him is present in his fears, life, and in his own name (White) when he is called Mr. Black by Colonel Aristotle Sesosteris of the Greek Royal Army. The symbiosis of opposites appears in his own identity when the political crisis of the foreign country resembles his:

> 'Ah. English, are you?'
> 'Yes, no, Irish'
> 'Irish? Ah.' (N., p.64)

---

[11] In his course "Postcolonial Theory and the Irish Novel", given at the University of São Paulo in 1994, Declan Kiberd used the term "troublemaker".

The author shows through the character-narrator the presence of the Other-within-himself. The Irish were obliged to become English by force and, even though they have now gained their independence from the coloniser in the south, they still use the invader's language which gives shape to their discourse. Consequently, their identity remains a double one. In "A Talk"[12] Banville discusses the tension produced by the English language in the Irish mind when the native Irish language was destroyed by the Penal Laws in the 18th century. Nevertheless, he doubts whether the Irish could have resisted the colonialism of the English language even if they had victoriously resisted the coloniser:

> Could we have resisted the colonialism of the English language, even if we had successfully resisted the colonisers themselves?
> I do not rejoice in the loss of a native language. But I would be hypocritical if I said that I do not rejoice in being an English speaker - or it would be more precise to say, in being a writer in English.[13]

This theme was to be analysed in his next novel, *Birchwood*.

Duality of identity could be associated with the determinism of the narrator's birth as a colonised subject, or, if we consider the genre of the novel as a *thriller*, with the stereotype of the treacherous revolutionary Irishman whose ambivalent attitude towards taking possession of the document changes the history of the Greek island. Finally, we could also associate it with his role as a disloyal narrator as I have already mentioned.

Ben White is also an important chess piece in the revolutionary game against the military coup. "Nightspawn" acquires another meaning: "the black pawn", the piece that goes first to the front but which has no knowledge of the plan that is being constructed by another mind, probably the knight, Mr Knight or Charles, nicknamed by the narrator as *"the knight of the night"* and *"the white knight"* simultaneously. He is also a "pawn" that follows the plan initially shaped by the narrator, creator of the story, before he loses control of it. There are many pawns

---

[12] In: *IUR*, Vol.11, No.1, 1981. pp.13-17
[13] ibid. p.14

on the chessboard of the narrative - Erik Weiss, Andreas, the sailors or *true mariners*, that are manipulated by circumstances as if they were marionettes. They appear and disappear without leaving any trace which might have enabled Ben White to have solved the enigma. The unfinished game, still set up on the chessboard at Julian Kyd's home is the image of the unfinished process of a narrative within another narrative (the narrator's within the author's) which is made up of successive events without any explanation. Many actions of the characters are reflections of the moves of the pieces on the chess board: *"White pawn to black king one. Look at this"* (168).

The narrator constantly declares that he has no control over the story and only silence and a re-start remain: another attempt to write or rather, to rewrite.

Nightspawn is a process within another process, the unsuccessful attempt to provide order within chaos in the act of narrating the past. Recollections become muddled in the narrator's memory, speeding through the tunnel of time and taking shape through insinuating metaphors. The narrator insists on *"this mixed bag of metaphors" (p.129)*. There are flashes of intertwined significations pointing out the very life that escapes explanation, echoing Beckett's conception of art.

In his first novel, Banville looks at ways in which we attempt to grasp the past and, at the impossibility of ordering facts, he questions the act of remembering due to the uncertainty that it generates. Ambiguity, one of the colonial discursive prints, reappears in his second novel with authority facing the incommunicability of the past in the eternal present of the writer.[14] In the act of narrating, the writer recreates this past which becomes his present since it is a construction of his own mind. This ambiguity recreated by the I shows the fallibility of memory and opens the way for reflection about human existence and thought: the modern *cogito*. Only re-readings of *"the statements of the past survive"*.

"Cogito ergo sum" in Reverse in the Light of Postcolonial Theory

In *Da Vanguarda ao Pós-Moderno*, Eduardo Subirats analyses Cartesian aesthetics and discusses its problematization within the cultural, historical and aesthetic aspects of modernism. Analogically, that tension between the negative and the positive, the destructive task of scepticism and the constructive task of self-reflective rationalism,[15] is questioned and even reversed by Banville to create an estrangement in the aesthetic field of fiction and to re-shape the very concept of fiction as the art of "doing".

Banville begins his polemic with the opening statement of *Birchwood*. The following statement reinforces the estrangement, showing the determinism of a postcolonial Ireland constructing itself in the context of metaphorical images employed throughout the first paragraph:

> I am, therefore I think. That seems inescapable. In this lawless house I spend the nights poring over my memories, fingering them, like an impotent casanova his old love letters, sniffing the dusty scent of violets. Some of these memories are in a language which I do not understand, the ones that could be headed, the beginning of the old life. They tell the story which I intend to copy here, all of it, if not its meaning, the story of the fall and rise of Birchwood, and of the part Sabatier and I played in the last battle. (B., p.11)

The need to go back to the origin, to start from zero again, is reframed in this paragraph, even the reversal of the Cartesian thought compels the reader to deconstruct not only the *epistemê* of Descartes's *cogito*, but also of the *modern cogito* proposed by Foucault which argues that Cartesian thought is that which is most generally responsible for error or illusion and which reveals the distance separating current thought from that which is rooted in the unthinkable.[16]

---

[14] See Laura Izarra, "*Birchwood*, The Incommunicable Past in the Eternal Present of John Banville". In: ANAIS DO XXI SENAPULLI, Maringá: UEM, 1989. pp.75-82.
[15] Eduardo Subirats, *Da Vanguarda ao Pós-Moderno, p.60*.
[16] Michel Foucault, *As palavras e as coisas. Uma arqueologia das ciências humanas*. p. 340.

According to Foucault, "I think" does not prove the truth of "I am". He goes on to reflect on the fact that human thought contemplates the unthinkable and seeks to articulate it. The *modern cogito* analyses human nature and questions its relationship with the unthinkable.

Banville reverses the Cartesian *cogito* in the light of Foucault's *modern cogito* to provoke a feeling of estrangement in the reader. Affirming Being before Thinking Banville stresses the existentialism of the human being, inviting us to make a postmodern reading of the human being within his socio-political context and in the light of his attempt to articulate the unthinkable, the *modern cogito*, as a supplement of the original - *the Cartesian cogito*.

This duality, according to Foucault, is very strange, and its role is to bring thought as near as possible to itself in order to disclose the Unconscious, to absorb its silence or its indefinite murmur.[17]

While postcolonial discourse creates a duality in counterpoint, modern thought turns to the Other of the human being which is engaged in a constant attempt to make itself the same as the human being. Both in *Birchwood* and *Nightspawn* the other exists in the political unconscious, implicit in the self, assuming either the role of one or the other in search of its "real" identity. Homi Bhabha calls this process "the moving frontier of alterity within identity".[18] Here the "self" is constituted by the traces of the Other. The "self" thus either identifies itself in terms of difference from the Other or rejects this alterity looking for self-affirmation. Banville portrays this tension, using the conflicting duality of his characters, while the power of the *modern cogito* is reversed to transform the passive attitude of the reader into action. He invokes the unthinkable - the being before the thinking - and "articulates" the silences within the socio-political context of contemporary Ireland. The existence that affirms the presence of

---

[17]Michel Foucault, *As palavras e as coisas. Uma arqueologia das ciências humanas.* P. 342
[18]Homi Bhabha, "The Other Question: Difference, Discrimination and the Discourse of Colonialism"; in: Bhabha, H. *Literature, Politics and Theory.* p.153.
& _____. "Interrogating Identity. Frantz Fanon and the Postcolonial Prerogative"; in _____ *The Location of Culture*, 1994. p.51.

thought in the unthinkable transforms itself into a dangerous act due to this very reversal because it reaffirms the interaction between silences and their context. This does not mean that Banville's writing may be described as *engagé*. Banville is against this idea, though in a recent interview he admitted the presence of a political context in *Birchwood:*

> I was surprised by how much of the Northern Troubles had crept into it, without my knowing. So, that book is representative of its time, but I didn't do it to be that way. And that is the absolutely crucial difference, between what you mean to do and what is done.[19]

The political unconscious is thus latent in Banville's creative process and it becomes manifest in the act of rereading when the "indefinite murmurs" of the writer's silence are heard and contextualized by the reader, influenced by the reversal of the Cartesian *cogito,* which interacts dialogically with the *modern cogito* - the emphasis on existence with the thought of the unthinkable.

The Postcolonial Discourse Implicit in *Birchwood*

In *A Short History of Irish Literature* Seamus Deane shows how *Birchwood* is narrated by the hero in the form of a memoir, in reversed time, set in the period of the Irish Civil War (1919-1921) and the Great Hunger in 1840. There are intertextual echoes of writers of those periods and the novel's form is similar to the genre of the "Big House" novels. In *Transitions: Narratives in Modern Irish Culture,* Richard Kearney argues that Banville parodies the traditional genre of the "Big House" satirising its *clichés*. Imhof reveals the unreality of fictional time related to historical facts and insists that *Birchwood* does not belong to the "big house" genre. It is, in his opinion, a Proustian novel in search of time lost, in search of the meaning of life. In this search, Banville uses different genres - the

---

[19] *HOT PRESS,* Vol.18, No.19, 5 October, 1994.

detective, Gothic and picaresque - combining circular and binary structures in the comic-heroic style of the eighteenth-century novel. I agree with some of Imhof's statements as they are the result of detailed structuralist analyses that help to elucidate many aspects of the writer's art. Nevertheless, I cannot share his reading of *Birchwood* as a picaresque novel because, although he points out the presence of picaresque elements in the narrative, he does not consider their function within the historical context of the genre. For example, contrary to what he affirms, the picaresque novel has a closed ending because the *pícaro*-narrator is not a *pícaro*-protagonist at the moment he starts narrating his memoirs. He is writing to justify his past actions because he has already attained a peak of social status when he becomes a writer. The picaresque novel is a satire upon society, as seen from the *pícaro*'s perspective, in which he portrays his initiation into the "school of life". The main movement of the novel is not horizontal (his adventures) but vertical: the social ascent of the protagonist together with his conscious moral descent or degradation; something that does not occur with Gabriel. He acquires a critical vision of the historical context but not of the different social scales (center and periphery) when he tours with the circus troup. On the other hand, he does not commit transgressions that degrade him morally.[20]

McMinn analyses the novel from the point of view of Gabriel Godkin's memoirs and focuses upon the symbolism present in the three parts of the book - "The Book of the Dead", "Air and Angels" and "Mercury" - which depict the search for beauty and harmony. These are represented in the first part through reversed images: the crippled nature of the birch wood itself, the broken glasses, the dead water of the broken fountain, the puzzle falling in pieces, the rhythm of the ball hitting the floor, the first attempt to ride a bicycle . . .

It is important to say that my analysis of *Birchwood* is not only based on its author's socio-historical background but also on my own position as a critical

---

[20] I have written a detailed study of the evolution of the picaresque genre and the Irish picaresque novel in my M.A. dissertation, *James Stephens: The Demi-Gods at the Crossroads*, 1988. (unpublished) A copy may be consulted at the National Library in Dublin.

Latin American reader able to empathise with Banville's political unconscious in its postcolonial Irish context. This unconscious was to assume other manifestations in his subsequent novels and was to interact with concepts of science and painting as he constructed his new aesthetic synthesis.

Gabriel Godkin, child of an incestuous love, narrates the decay and rebirth of the "Big House", symbol of the Protestant Ascendancy in Ireland. Representing both the apogee and the decadence of a declining empire, this symbol, together with the pre-colonial Celtic heroes, inspired the Irish Renaissance led by Yeats. Gabriel searches for his identity, attempting to comprehend the past despite its incommunicability. In the novel, the past expresses itself through an unknown language that the narrator tries to reproduce without understanding it, following the *modern cogito* way of thinking. The search for the "self" is represented by the search for the Other, his twin "sister" (who turns out to be a twin brother, Michael, whose existence is unknown till Gabriel becomes aware of him when he returns to his mansion in the third part of the book and finds him taking part in the civil war fighting against his own family roots).

In my opinion, the novel is a historical allegory of colonial Ireland, in which the *"twin-within-himself"*, a device present in most of Banville's novels, is not only a representation of the division between Protestant and/or English and Catholic and/or Irish, but also of the "fusion" of both cultures - the coloniser embodies the colonised, the oppressed embodies the oppressor. In his story of a fictional family, Banville also narrates part of the history of the northern conflicts in his country - The Troubles.

The *Lawless* house, the anarchic baroque house invaded by the peasants, is the centre of the first part of the circular structure of the novel, entitled "The Book of the Dead". The title is an allusion to the Egyptian mortuary verses that guided the dead on their journey to salvation. In the last part of the novel it acquires a metaphorical meaning as Gabriel's memories become his guide in his attempt to understand the incommunicable past and foresee his future. However, the sign is stripped of its meaning when the narrator's memory fails as he is retelling his past. There is thus no salvation for him in his art of writing.

> I could no longer remember what she looked like. How many have I lost that way? I began to write as a means of finding them again, and thought that at last I had discovered a form which would contain and order all my losses. I was wrong. There is no form, no order, only echoes and coincidences, sleight of hand, dark laughter. I accept it.(*B.*, p.174)

The past belongs to the dead and it is incommunicable. Throughout the book's disordered narrative, historical flashbacks mix with personal experiences which reflect the divided self in an equally divided and paradoxal microcosm, where chaos is opposed to the illusion of order. The context, the "wild country" and its "natives", does not represent decadence, as was the case in colonial discourse. The narrator selects reminiscences which prove that, on the contrary, decay started in the very heart of the new Ascendancy family. This has the politico-historical connotation that the natives could not be held responsible for the decay of their country and emphasises the decadence in the coloniser's inner being.

Birchwood, the Big House, belonged to Gabriel's mother's family, the *Lawlesses*, who represent the social class made up of the first English colonisers born in Ireland, the "Old English" and who, according to the English, had their "ethos" corrupted by contact with the natives. When the narrator introduces his mother, he says, *"She was a Lawless, and for such a sin there was no forgiveness"* (15).

At the opening of the novel, the mansion has just been "conquered" by the *Godkins*, Gabriel's father's family, who represent the "New English":

> Where he (Gabriel Godkin, his great-great-grandfather) came from is not known, nor who he was. One day, suddenly, he was here, and nothing was the same again. (*B.*, p.15)

When the New English came to Ireland, they redistributed the properties belonging to the Old English by purchase for investment purposes, marriage with members of the Irish aristocracy, or by appropriation, protected by the colonial laws (the Penal Laws). The Protestants had the right to claim as their own any lands belonging to Catholics who had not converted into Anglicanism. Traditional land-owners like the Lawlesses were obliged to go to the cities and devote themselves to commerce. Sometimes they managed to recover their former property in settlement of debts due to the bad administration of the new owners, as happens in the novel. Subsequently, during the civil war, the peasants took possession of the last few Big Houses, destroying them and reaffirming the state of "chaos" never understood by the coloniser.

The socio-political context portrayed in *Birchwood* shows how the coloniser confronted evidence of an unfinished conquest in the Irish land and the identity conflicts that this evidence provoked not only in the colonised but, more specifically, in the Ascendancy. In Chapter Eight of *Modern Ireland 1600-1972*, "The Ascendancy Mind", R.F. Foster quotes Daniel Corkery's reminder, in *The Hidden Ireland*, that the mind of the Ascendancy is not the same as that of the English. Foster explains that, in the eighteenth century, membership of the Ascendancy was not restricted to English descendants and Protestants. The Ascendancy at that time resembled Anglicanism, which not only draws from the social elite, but also from the rural and professional classes descended from the Normans, the "Old English, Cromwell himself and, in some rare cases, from the Gaels. Thus, the Ascendancy did not have a particular ethnic origin, although it shared the characteristic of *exclusivity* that distinguishes Anglicanism. It was composed of an elite that monopolised legislation, politics and society, and whose aspirations were focused on the Irish House of Commons.[21] The Ascendancy thus formed an aristocracy of "self-made-men" with a political conscience of superiority in relation to the native Irishmen and also with strong feelings of suspicion concerning any British measures that might break their monopoly. They

---

[21]Roy F. Foster. *op.cit.*, pp. 170-173.

spoke in the name of Ireland as if theirs were the only voice of "their country"; other voices were completely silenced.

In the first part of the novel Banville portrays this nationalist colonial context where the natives (the peasants) were seen as barbarian only because the English failed to understand both their unfixed structures of economic relations and their election system of land ownership which was contrary to the European heredity system, as Foster mentions.[22] The paradoxal relationship between the initial superiority and subsequent decadence of the aristocratic class of the Ascendancy is perfectly rendered in the narrator's casual yet ironic discourse when he refers to the natives:

> The final proof, the clincher, as they say, that the Godkins were going the way of all the gentry, that is down, was the newfound boldness of the peasants. As my people knew, and lucky they did, there is nothing that will keep the Irish in their place like a well-appointed mansion. They may despise and hate you, only put a fine big house with plenty of windows in it up on a hill and bejapers you have them be the balls, stunned into a cringing, cap-touching coma. But beware. It is a fragile thraldom. The first unmended fence will mean the first snigger behind your back outside the chapel yard, an overrun garden will bring them grinning to the gate, and a roof left in visible disrepair will see them poaching your land in daylight, as now they poached ours, contemptuous not only of the law but even of my father's shotgun, which was no mean threat. (*B.*, p.50)

The voraciousness of time corroding ever faster the mansion and its inhabitants, and the unthought deaths outside the natural compass of time set the protagonist's reflection against the background symphony of sounds that represent metonymically the slow rhytm of decay in his own home:

> Of course our genteel slide toward penury was never mentioned, not in my presence, but the silent evidence of it was everywhere around me, in the cracked paint and the missing tiles, the dry rot that ate its way unchecked across the floors and up the stairs, in the games of musical chairs which Mama played, switching them from the front rooms to the back in a circle of

---

[22] Roy F. FOSTER. *Modern Ireland 1600-1972*. p.9

increasing degeneracy until the day when, groaning and creaking, they regained their original places and the wheel ceased to turn. (*B.*, p.49)

The style and images chosen by the writer expand the significations of the text. For example, the long open vowel sounds become shorter and mix with the plosive consonants and sibilant sounds which, together with the nasal endings of the verbs, reproduce onomatopoeically the vibration and disintegration of rot and decadence.

Banville also describes the fear that the natives exercised over the narrator when he was a child and went into the woods with Michael, *"I felt a mingled excitement and dread, and a sensation of controlled and not unpleasant panic"* (54).

Little by little this feeling transforms itself into incomprehension and moves him to adopt a paternalistic attitude at the end of the novel. The philanthropic image of assisting the weak is typical of the coloniser who needs to see the colonised as dependent and subservient in order to affirm his own sense of superiority.

> I watch from my window, fascinated. I wanted to go and help them, to say, *Look, I am not my father, I am something different*, but they would have run away from me, horrified.
> . . . Outside is destruction and decay. I do not speak the language of this wild country. I shall stay here, alone, and live a life different from any the house has ever known. Yes. (*B.*, p.174)

But the discourse is self-defensive moulding the Anglo-Irish identity of the character through the negation of the coloniser and the stereotypical images of the Irish natives - barbarians and pagans. Paradoxically, it reaffirms the stereotype of a wild country due to the estrangement produced by the coloniser's language. The novel's discourse belongs to the exclusion zone of the oppressor, who cannot penetrate the conspiracy against him in the specific historical moment portrayed in the novel - the civil war. In this case, the Other is vulnerable because the oppressed was forced to use the coloniser's language and thus had direct access to his code, a process which does not happen in reverse. In Banville's political unconscious, the dominant and treacherous attitude of the coloniser - *"that glorious record of deaths and treachery"* - and the treacherous subservience of the colonised amalgamate in the process of a new self-definition. The presence of one in the other is the *supplement* in the construction of a new identity which is not static but dynamic and in constant formation.

The names of the family represent the stereotyped images of the colonised. The natives are seen by the domineering ideology as anarchists due to the simple fact that they redefine the state of ownership of a property every generation, which is contrary to the European centralised form of heredity as I have already mentioned. The natives "contaminated" the "Old English", represented by the *Lawlesses*, who incorporated the fragmented power of the English born in Ireland. The *Godkins*, "God's descendants", embody the divine connotation that the Ascendancy acquires in the theological and political fields as being "the chosen", as opposed to those Irish natives who refused to convert to Anglicanism and thus lost the ownership of their properties. Anglocentricism and the aggressive spirit of Protestantism provoked a crisis of identity in the "Old English", who were pushed out into the exclusion zone together with the natives upon the arrival of "New English", who represent the new class of landowners introduced by the Tudors. This gave rise to the tension of identities in the plantation culture, which provided the seed for the Anglo-Irishness portrayed by the narrator in its duality and amalgamation.

Having analysed the historical roots of the stereotypes deconstructed by Banville in *Birchwood*, it may be helpful to recall Menezes de Souza's critical comment on how Bhabha sees the stereotype in counter-discursive practice. Drawing on psychoanalysis, Menezes de Souza argues that the stereotype is a *fetish*, *"something psychologically contradictory because it represents the desire for totality/an absent completion, and simultaneously, reminds the absence/lack of that same totality/completion."* [23] Banville declared to Imhof in an interview that his characters are stereotypes drawn from the "Big House" novel genre, *"the overbearing father, long-suffering mother, sensitive son, and then also other strands, the quest, the lost child, the doppelgänger".*[24]

In Banville's selection of names for his characters, he subverts the stereotype as fetish, showing through silence the need for the stereotype to be present in order to self-define and understand its origin and subsequently destroy it. The function of the stereotype is not related to the desire for completion. Mirroring the lack of the other, the deformities of the stereotype acquire exaggerated dimensions, contradicting its own referentiality and provoking self-negation in its distorted reflexion.

Thus, discourse analysis reveals that *Birchwood* is more than a mere parody of the "Big House" novel as Kearney and Imhof argued. The stereotyped characters invert their roles; they become tragic in their comicality, and acquire a political dimension within the process of defamiliarization. The colonial discourse that stereotyped the colonised turns against the colonisers themselves when multiple identities from the collective unconscious start interacting in the construction of a new postcolonial identity. This inversion takes place in the second part of the novel and introduces the possibility of a transcendental mutual understanding in the last part.

According to McMinn, Banville explores the mystery of the harmony between the physical and the spiritual world in "Air and Angels", echoing the following lines from John Donne's love poem "Aire and Angels":

> Then as an Angel, face and wings
> Of aire, not pure as it, yet pure doth eare,
> So thy love may be my loves spheare;
> Just such disparitie
> As is twixt Aire and Angells puritie,
> 'Twixt womens love, and mens will ever be.

---

[23] Lynn M. Menezes de Souza. "O rato que ruge: o discurso crítico-literário pós-colonial como suplemento. In: *CROP*, No.1. p.64.
[24] *IUR*, Vol.11, No.1, 1981. p.11.

In my opinion, the second part of the novel describes colonial encounters *per se*: the Anglo-Irish relate both to the magic world of the coloniser and to the land of the colonised in the process of formation. In order to understand its title it is helpful to recall Walter Benjamin's allegory of progress based on Klee's painting "Angelus Novus".[25] The angel has his face turned towards the past, trying to awaken the dead and reconstruct what has been destroyed; but the storm called progress is pushing him violently back towards the future while a pile of debris rises to the skies. Banville's angel, Gabriel (man of God), tries to understand and reconstruct the past in order to find an exit from his eternal present and start to construct a new future. But the air (literature) pushes him towards an unknown future allowing him to do no more than observe the fragmented past. Banville thus portrays the tension between the usurper/oppressor and the usurped/oppressed and the internal conflicts generated in the region of the unthinkable: the process of formation of the Anglo-Irish identity.

The protagonist escapes from home the night before he is to be sent to boarding school and he narrates how he joined a circus, a world which realises its own fantasies. The public wishes to be deceived and conspires with the performers, paying to believe in the fantasy they create, *"they **pay**, mark you, and their pennies work like magic wands, transforming all they buy"* (108).

Metaphors construct the narrative signification of the second part of the novel, diverging from the expectations raised by the name of the circus - *PROSPERO'S MAGIC CIRCUS*. The circus promises entertainment and even has the approval of the Queen:

> 'WE WERE AMUSED'
> HRH
> The Queen

---

[25] Walter Benjamin, "Sobre o conceito da história". In: *Walter Benjamin. Obras Escolhidas. Magia e técnica, arte e política.* Editora Brasiliense, 1986. p.226.

The narrator perceives that the circus is another *"collapsible kingdom"* and he feels betrayed by this discovery. Nevertheless, he is seduced by the everyday unreality and reacts in the same way as the public, becoming another player in the game of enchanters and enchanted.

In fact, Prospero's Magic Circus is more travelling theater than circus. The major attraction is a stuffed *"motheaten tiger lying motionless behind bamboo bars on a trailer"*; the grey tubercular and skinny monkey is in a birdcage. The hyper-reality of the show is created magically by the spectator rather than by the creator of the fantasy.

> 'It is *real*, you know, Gabriel. They find it quite convincing'.
> *They* were the folk who paid to look upon these wonders. There was both mockery and reverence in the way he spoke the word. People believed the shoddy dreams he sold them! The fact filled him with awe. (*B.*, p.108)

PROSPERO'S MAGIC CIRCUS is of course a direct reference to Shakespeare's *The Tempest*, in which Prospero is a foreign visitor to the island, in time becoming a magic coloniser, while Caliban, the native host, is deprived of his rights and becomes a slave. The analogies and irony are evident in *Birchwood*, especially when Silas and Gabriel's farce takes place within a larger farce, the narrator's, an echo of Prospero's play within Shakespeare's. In the fraudulent session of hypnotism, Silas, the leader of the group, transfers the supernatural power of the grey monkey to himself to dominate the will of the world, and hypnotises Gabriel into doing everything he orders. The dialogic exchanges reinforce the relationship of dependence *master/slave*:

> 'Come, you cannot resist me.', 'Master, I am your slave, do with me what you could.', 'Ladies and gentlemen, what shall I have him do, my slave?' . . . 'Would, not could, you clown.'(*B.*, p.115)

Nevertheless, the resistance of the oppressed is implicitly revealed when Gabriel, whilst supposedly under the fake hypnotic effect, forgets the previously rehearsed lines and answers to Silas's commands *"Master, I am your slave, do with me what you could"* instead of *"would"*. This sketch not only refers to the first need of the coloniser, that of being fed by the colonised (as Peter Hulme affirms in *Colonial Encounters)*, but also to the need of the coloniser to show publicly how he has exercised his power over his subordinate through the latter's unconditional obedience.

The names of the actors in the farce permit different readings if we consider that the artistic name of Gabriel (Johann Livelb) is an anagram of John Banville, a writer who feels himself colonized due to the historical process of appropriating the language of the "other", a manipulation of "free will". Albert, the monkey's name, can be seen as an irreverent allusion to the royal family if a historical relationship is established between the Great Hunger and the advertisement of the circus:

> PROSPERO'S MAGIC CIRCUS
> by appointment to the
> CROWNED HEADS OF EUROPE
> ....
> 'WE WERE AMUSED'
> HRH
> The Queen

Albert, Prince of Germany, spouse and main counsellor of Queen Victoria, was the royal husband who has exercised most power in the British Crown since 1840. In a parodic act, Silas holds his hand over the monkey's bald head to transfer all its power to himself before the session of hypnotism. Prospero is the unnameable, the absence in presence, who paradoxically provokes absolute silence or fantastic references to his prosperity and physical appearance. It is in this way that Banville subverts the stereotype as a fetish and creates a stereotype of the "other" in relation to his own image:

> I like to imagine him as a tiny withered old man with skin like wrinkled brown paper, sparrow hands, a big hat, a cloak, a crooked stick, pale piercing eyes, always before me, like a black spider, his bent back, the tapping stick, leading me ever on into a mysterious white landscape. I knew that picture was all wrong, but it sufficed. (*B.*, p.118)

This description reveals numerous political and psychological connotations through its overuse of metaphorical images, which might so saturate the reader's interpretation that he/she could be led to believe that the postcolonial perspective presented here is also stereotyped. But denying that stereotype affirms the existence of a present absence. The reader may therefore choose how to interpret this caricaturised passage, which is an echo of the stereotyped image of the Irish in the colonial period when they were compared to monkeys and black images. It should be remembered that the reference to Prospero's absence/presence represents the "new English" who, having taken possession of their Irish lands spend most of their time in England, exercising their power from abroad. This hidden mythical power generated by absence produces a feeling of estrangement and creates infinite possibilities:

> There was something always ahead of us, a nameless promise never reached and yet always within reaching distance. (*B.*, p.125)

The names of the other members of the travelling theatre also serve as metaphors for the colonial condition: Silas, an abbreviation for Silvanus (latin) - "god of the woods" - leads the group that takes fantasy from town to town and dominates people (audience and circus performers alike) in their own space. His wife's name, Sybil (Greek), carries a double meaning - prophetess and "counselled by divinity". Magnus, the greatest, is a clown and Gabriel's best friend. Gabriel identifies with him because of his sadness and the liberating effect of his laughter. Rainbird, an illusionist and magician, and Angel, the guardian angel and cook, who after long hours of travelling or work, helps the performers to recover from cold and exhaustion with hot soups and teas, both create the illusion of home in the cramped old tent. Mario, the juggler, is the handsome, romantic figure who is loved by the twins Ada (Hebrew) and Ida (German). Banville uses the image of twins in many of his novels, but in this case the twins are female. They are physically alike but spiritually different. The former, beautiful and cruel, is a voracious eater and represents the five senses in extreme.

On the other hand, Ida represents gentle youth with her childlike appearance and her wonder concerning the natural world and the unknown. She dies victim of the violent abuse of the soldiers. The two girls are the stereotyped allegorical images of England and Ireland respectively.

Silas and Sybil's children are also twins, though they are identical and androgenous. Their monstrous physical appearance frightens Gabriel:

> They were an uncanny, disturbing couple. In spite of their difference in gender, which was minimal anyway, they were doubles in body and spirit, a beautiful two-headed monster, wicked, destructive, unfailingly gay. Magnus merged them into a single entity which he called Justinette. He had the right idea. I was afraid of them. (*B.*, p.119)

What provokes the Gothic horror in Gabriel is not only the anomalous physical union of two human beings into the one being that Magnus called "Justinette", but also the very symbol of hybridity that they represent: the fusion of two cultures dominated by stereotypes. The twins represent the fear of an absolute loss of identity in the fusion of two foreign cultures which become identical in the dark abyss of hybridity. In the third part of the novel hybridity acquires further dimension, symbolised by the image of Mercury.

The Great Hunger is the historical period brought into the narrator's present in the second part of *Birchwood*. He denounces what will be always the greatest abyss in Anglo-Irish history, the unsurmounted barrier of conciliation.

> As news of the blight spread, only marginally swifter than the blight itself, the fields were stripped, and what was left, the great meadows of corn, the cattle, these were reserved for export to another land, and trade would not be disrupted or even interrupted because of a mere famine. The first deaths were reported as the grainships sailed. (*B.*, p.140)

The cruelty of the historical moment described in the passage above is printed with blood in the Irish memory, an *"intimation"* surviving from the past which must be exorcised through writing. When Sybil becomes ill with sadness, the narrator says that the cause is the country's sadness, as if that too had possessed her soul against her will. The description of people starving is dramatic - *"baffled people in the rotting fields, of the stricken eyes staring out of hovels"* (143).

As the performers travel they hear stories that people used to eat grass, the bark of trees, dried leaves and even mud. Chaos gripped the country: bands of hermaphrodites robbed, killed and, it was said, even ate their victims. The horror generated by this cannibalistic image, an echo of Caliban in *The Tempest*, obliges the narrator to justify the exaggeration as a game to keep reality at bay. But reality was hunger and the only palliative was the invention of tall stories to neutralise the truth of it.

At the beginning of the novel, the narrator recalls the echoes of the Great Hunger from the past, which fuse with the one he himself witnesses to make it an atemporal historical fact, an eternal present in his mind. Looking at the past with an ironic eye he reveals the relationship between the oppressed and the oppressor:

> He (Joseph Lawless) is remembered in our annals for his answer to the commissioner who informed him at the height of a potato famine that the tenants of Birchwood were being decimated by starvation. *A trick, sir, another of their tricks!* Joseph roared. Indeed he was right, was Joseph, for the peasants were a tricky lot, they died by the score, thereby forcing the authorities across the sea to send in a relief shipment of six sacks of Indian corn. (*B.*, p.15)

The narrator's irony thus subverts another colonial stereotype transforming it into a tragic one.

The third part of *Birchwood*, is the "solution" to the problem introduced in the first part, thus closing the circular structure of the narrative. When Imhof mentions to Banville that the book ends like a detective novel, the writer both affirms and denies this, *"I like the end of Birchwood, where everything is wrapped up, and nothing is wrapped up"*.[26]

---

[26]*IUR*, Vol.11, No.1, 1981. p. 11.

This ambiguous answer refutes the closure of the detective story in favour of the postmodern tendency to offer alternatives, to leave an opening which will enable the reader to see various possible endings to the narrative.

At the end of the novel, Gabriel escapes from the circus and wanders alone, surviving thanks to the charity of the poor. Without knowing it, he walks in a circle with the circus at its centre. Metonymically, the mythical image of England continues to be the centralising force in the mind of the Ascendancy. It is the European model in the formation of a new identity.

Gabriel returns to the mansion and perceives that his "collapsible kingdom" has changed although it is ostensibly the same as it had been in the past. The peasants are fighting for their right to the land they have won with their work and they kill the only available representative of authority - Gabriel's father, Joseph Godkin.

When Gabriel chooses to stay in his collapsed kingdom he becomes Caligula from Silas's point of view, who had offered him the chance to return to the kingdom of fantasy. Gabriel struggles against the prejudice that labels him as autocratic, cruel and immoral for assuming his right to stay and construct a new meaning for Birchwood, the family mansion and symbol of the power of the Ascendancy in Ireland. His awareness of the presence of his twin brother is accompanied by a desire to kill him, to deny the fruit of incest and the implicit meaning of belonging to the Ascendancy (there was no drop of Irish/Old English blood running in his veins). But the force of continuity is finally stronger and he accepts the necessity of living with the menace of his brother's presence.

By the end of the novel, all the beliefs that had guided Gabriel in his search for an identity in the second part of the narrative have been transformed into broken glass, but each piece still retains the brightness of the fantasy he had created in order not to forget the past and to keep his hopes high.

> There is no girl. There never is. I suppose I always knew that, in my heart. I believed in a sister in order not to believe in **him**, my cold mad brother. No Prospero either, there never is. O but I so wanted to keep that withered wizard, with his cloak and his black hat, stumping on ahead of me always

> with his stick and his claw and his piercing eyes, leading me slowly toward that rosy grail. Now the white landscape was empty. Perhaps it is better thus, I said, and added, faintly, I might find other creatures to inhabit it. And I did, and so I became my own Prospero, and yours. (*B*., p.172)

It is self-affirmation not external models which will mould his new identity, simultaneously reflecting a leadership quality that will turn him into a model to be followed himself. The past is thus shown to return eternally.

The third part of the novel acquires a transcendental and ambiguous dimension in association with its title "Mercury". Like the classical Mercury (Hermes in Greek mythology), who was the messenger of the gods and a guide for selves in their changes of state, Banville's messenger Gabriel, introduces himself, with all his eloquence, maturity and sagacity, to be the guide and mediator in the process of construction of a new Anglo-Irish identity. He acquires the mythical significance of an inner judge (conscience) of a race, diving deep into its consciousness to show the people wisdom and the way to self-awareness. Where the classical god's winged sandals signified his powers of flight and swift movement,[27] Gabriel's wanderings with the circus and his critical self-awareness have a similar symbolism.

In Roman mythology, Mercury receives from Apollo the gifts of foresight and a golden caduceus, a magic wand with two embattled snakes twisting around it in opposite directions. The snakes represent primordial chaos when they fight and its polarization when they are separated by Mercury; their twisting symbolises the equilibrium of opposite tendencies around the same axis, which implies that Mercury's caduceus is a symbol of peace.[28] Analogically, Gabriel possesses similar attributes and succeeds in magically polarising the two powers in conflict, the twins (Foucault's Other in oneself), so that equilibrium can be achieved within the dualistic Anglo-Irish nature as it was in the myth. Gabriel becomes the god of mystery and of the art of decoding it.

---

[27] Jean Chevalier A. Gheerbrant. *Dicionário de Símbolos*, p.487.
[28] Ibid. p. 160.

The narrator, assuming the role of Prospero - oppressor and oppressed -, becomes a prophet who unveils those ambiguous inner conflicts that provoke changes of identity. Without any answer and echoing Wittgenstein's words *"whereof I cannot speak, thereof I must be silent"* (as some secrets cannot be revealed), the writer metaphorically deconstructs an alternative: the return to a universal symbol taken from alchemy, mercury, which is "a solution, a regression to an non-differentiated state".[29] Thus, the process symbolises a tendency towards hybridity. But, if mercury has the power to purify and fix gold, if it is a science of interior regeneration, Banville, analogically, tries to demonstrate in *Birchwood* the possibility of human regeneration and liberation from the seduction of subjectivity and to show that man can adapt to external needs despite the pressure of his inner duality.

The Function of the Comic and the Grotesque in Postcolonial Discourse

Analysing Banville's first novels is a challenge because each one is a seed that will germinate separately in each of the following ones. There can be no doubt that Banville follows the traditional rules of nineteenth-century novels only to reverse their conventions and provoke a tension in the reader who, facing the lack of verisimilitude, suffers the dislocation from his/her belief in "realist" fiction to the presence of "a true fiction".

Two questions arose from my reading of the first two novels and guided me in my attempt to elucidate the *new synthesis* proposed by Banville: how does the writer experiment with and subvert the autobiographical mode in the voice of the narrator epitomised in *The Book of Evidence* and *Ghosts*? and, how does Banville break the intimate relationship between reader and writer when he introduces a grotesque and comic touch at the most tragic moments of the narrative? This break produces an ironic tension whose function appears to be to suspend the

---
[29]*Ibid.*, p. 607.

reader's involvement which is simultaneously offered and refused by the writer himself. Banville uses this technique in all his novels, introducing himself as a comic writer in the tragedy of thought.[30]

An interesting example is Ben White's first encounter with death in *Nightspawn*. This occurs when he is in the square in the suffocating heat of midday. A fat man running in his direction is shot in front of him. There is a grotesque description of the mortally injured man. The language used by the writer recalls the idea of a wounded animal, and creates a dramatic but subverted tone when the fall of the man is described as a circus pirouette which is followed by the dramatic force of the verb "crashed". The sensationalism of the "black blood" running down his wound is counterpoised by the description of contents of his pockets spread out on the ground and the idyllic image of a bird singing. The narrator uses sarcasm and irony to describe his own reaction to the scene:

> I did not move. It was not that I could not move, no, none of your paralysis of shock or any of that nonsense, just, I did not move. I was waiting for something.... Once again my patience had its prize. It must have been one of my better days. (*N.*, p. 21)

The episode ends with the grotesque portrait of the dead man lying ridiculously on the ground, in which the sublimity of being alive is contrasted with the absurdity of death:

> The fat felled man lay on his back with his legs flung wide and both arms trapped under him. One of his shoes had come off, and stood now beside the deserted foot, where a plump pink toe sprouted from a hole in the sock. He wore a baggy pair of trousers, and a gay red shirt, across which a troupe of dusky maidens danced, evoking the far south seas. His spectacles, shattered, dangled from his ear, and his wide eyes stared heedlessly at the luminous sky. There was a neat round puncture in his chest, which left a dancing girl decapitated, and a second ragged mouth gaped in his throat, marking the last bullet's exit. His attitude was one of extreme embarrassment, at being caught in such a helpless and undignified position. An angry red stain was

---

[30]Banville confirmed this idea in an interview he gave to me in April 1992.

> spreading beneath him in the dust, and an ant with a broken leg staggered through the mire. (*N.*, p.22)

The hole in the man's sock leaving his pink toe free, the "puncture" in his chest showing a decapitated dancing girl and the metaphorical image of a second mouth in his throat combine to produce a grotesque symbolic drama. The uncomfortable attitude of his inert body is witnessed by an ant, the universal symbol of industrious activity and also, in the Celtic tradition, of dedicated, untiring service. The hole, symbol of an opening to the unknown, is linked to fertility on the biological plane, to spirituality on the psychological one and to the birth of ideas on the intellectual one. In this way, Banville offers the reader a new conception of art together with the formation of a new political identity.

The tragi-comic is also present in *Birchwood* in the narrator's various descriptions of death, particularly that of the grandmother, who dies of self-combustion leaving only her feet in their scorched boots.

> ... I can never think of that ghastly day without suspecting that somewhere inside me some cruel little brute, a manikin in my mirror, is bent double with laughter. Granny! Forgive me. (*B.*, p.77).

Later, when Gabriel is in the travelling theatre, he discovers that soundless laughter is the link between the artists, the tragic silence of the comic.

> Laughter! O wicked, mind you, and vicious perhaps, but laughter for all that. And now I laughed too, but, like theirs, my laughter made no sound, no sound at all. (*B.*, p.107)

The sounds of silence materialised by the ambiguity of the colonial discourse create a polyphony in the field of the inverted *modern cogito*, suggesting that the discourse of Banville's first novels is a discourse in formation.

The ambivalence present at the beginning of the formation process of this new aesthetic synthesis, whether or not the fusion reaffirms the Anglo-Irish identity, was to be exorcised in the following novels through stereotypes. These stereotypes were always to be deconstructed from the perspective of interrelations between Science and Literature, or History, Painting and Literature, in such a way as to reveal their aesthetic function within the process, using either biographical or autobiographical discourse.

Banville's achievement in this first phase of his career was the successful definition of his awareness of the meaning of Art. He contested the limits of the nineteenth-century novel, perceiving that the intensity of a work of art turns the real into supra-reality, a construction of the artist's imagination. He fought the system from within, introducing familiar plots and characters in order *"to get through to a fairly large section of population."* [31] However, his failure was that he did not appeal to a wider public.

His subsequent novels focused on historical people in order to demonstrate parodically that, though real facts exist behind the lives of the scientists portrayed by the writer, the reader will not believe them because they are fiction - *"Because a novelist has no business taking actual historically recorded fact."* [32]

---

[31] Ronan Sheehan, "Novelists on the Novel". In: *The Crane Bag,* 3:1, 1979.p.81
[32] *Ibid.,* p. 83.

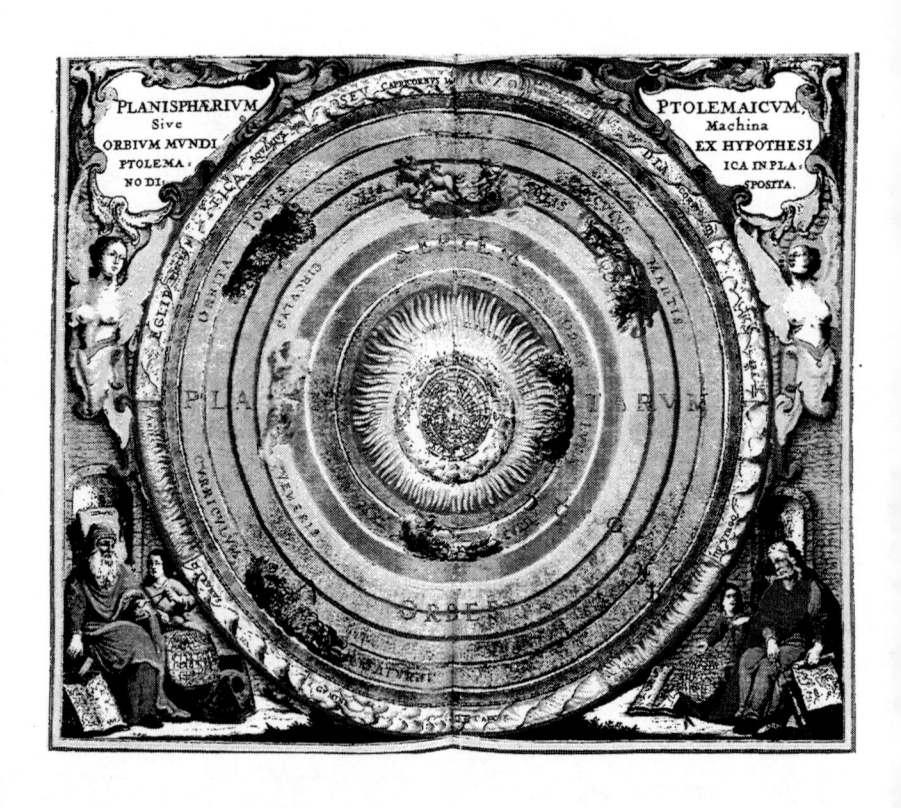

A Ptolemaic Map of the World.

Andreas Cellarius, *Atlas Coelestis seu Harmonia Macrocosmica* (Amsterdam, 1660).

Copperplate engraving on paper, hand colored.

Published by Pomegranate Publications, Petaluma, CA. The British Library, London, 1990

II

SCIENCE AND FICTION

> "There are implications in modern physics that affect our whole concept of reality. Modern atomic physics, for instance, seems to be pointing to the conclusion that there's no such things as matter, nothing *hard* . That atoms are some kind of energy waves - think of the philosophical implications of that!
> I'm interested in the way scientists 'do' science. It's a bit rather like the way artists do art."
> John Banville - *"Nothing to say!"*

A Dialogic Encounter Between Science and Literature

Despite the fact that new discoveries in Physics have provoked profound changes in our perception of the world, science, as one of the various manifestations of society, is still considered to be an independent and isolated variable. This assumption results from a system that has an internal logic, governed by its own rules, which validate a "reality" (an experience) separated from its context. The human mind has always seen science as representing natural phenomena in an objective and "truthful" way, because the information that it manipulates is obtained from controlled and quantitative observation. The scientist discovers within the apparent chaos of the universe an invisible order and transforms this into knowledge using a specific, precise and linear language, unshaded by ambiguity. But the myth that science is able to produce an objective, ideologically uncontaminated discourse, starts to be contested within its own field when it occurs with the veracity of historical discourse.

In the struggle to apprehend new truths, scientists have always had difficulty in expressing basic concepts because language and paradigms were generally inadequate to describe the phenomena observed. Their theories contested the visible and their minds formulated, *a priori* or *a posteriori*, syntheses that became supreme fictions, because a new vision of reality requires new syntheses and an appropriate language to represent it.

John Banville wrote *Doctor Copernicus* (1976), *Kepler* (1981), *The Newton Letter* (1982) and *Mefisto* (1986) upon the principles of a Greek tetralogy, three tragedies and a satire (*The Newton Letter*). According to him, the latter is *"a novella, set in the present, short, quite slight, very much an interlude in the tetralogy"*.[1]

Banville explored other roads for more than ten years in his search for a new, epistemological, vision of literary art, and he questioned diachronically the processes of the syntheses produced by the scientific revolutions. In his view, such revolutions produced new perceptions of the world, forming new meanings in the field of knowledge which, in their turn, influenced other fields, giving rise to new trends in writing and criticism in the realm of fiction. At the crossroads between Physics and Fiction, Banville seeks to reactivate a formerly incompatible theme - the relationship between science and literature in the context of a post-industrial society,[2] where the apogee of technology and communication theories allows a new form of representation: the concept of postmodern art.

As I mentioned previously in my Introduction, my aim here is to establish co-relations in the formation of concepts, chains of enunciations, and discursive and narrative formations, in order to visualise better the process of a new synthesis in

---

[1] *IUR*, Vol.11, No.1, 1981. p.12
[2] Alvin Toffler calls the post-industrial society "the third wave". He makes a detailed analysis of the world's economic and socio-political movements in his book *The Third Wave* (1980).

the art of writing. Banville deconstructs the illusory antagonism that presents science and literature as opposite discursive practices: the former as objective-descriptive, the latter as subjective-poetic. The nature of both creative processes becomes one: signs and images appear in the mind of both scientist and artist, shaping structures of signification, which language translates, in an orderly and intelligible way, within a context that mirrors the original chaos.

Banville perceives that both fields construct paradigms of reality; both aim to "represent", to control nature, in the sense of describing the universe (the physical and the human realms) in order to form and to record knowledge of the world. For Banville, the scientific imagination knits together "supreme fictions" in its attempt to "save the appearances/ the phenomena" of the old days and to explain facts in the light of the advent of modern science. He affirms that the scientific process of "creation" resembles the artistic process of imagination. Scientists *"do"* science in the same way that artists *"do"* art. Although conventional wisdom sees science as logical progression, there has been a lot of chance, of lucky mistakes, in the work of scientists.[3]

> A hidden theme of the series (the tetralogy) is the similarity between the workings of the artistic mind and the scientific mind; indeed, I sometimes feel that one could substitute the word "identity" for "similarity".[4]

Recent critical literary studies have focused on Blake and his perception of science, eighteenth-century poems representing periods of scientific discoveries, Romanticism and the evolution of species, the twentieth century and psychoanalytic theory. In recent decades various critics have narrowed the gap between literature and science, analysing the interaction between "the two cultures". Many critical tendencies have appeared since the well-known controversy between C.P. Snow and F.R. Leavis in the 60s provoked by Snow's

---

[3] "Nothing to Say!" & Rüdiger Imhof, "Question & Answer with John Banville". In: *ILS*, Sring 1987, p13
[4] *Ibid.*, p.13

famous lecture "The Two Cultures". Aldous Huxley's provocative book[5] concerning the impact of science and technology on Literature and Humanities, itself a reaction against Thomas Henry Huxley's proposal in favor of scientific education, advocated a synthesis that would link the scientific process to human values. Huxley's book complemented Matthew Arnold's essay[6] in which the term Literature was used in its widest sense, not only as *belles lettres* but also as a mode that contains all knowledge generated by human interest. For example, according to Arnold, the scientific results published by Copernicus, Galileu, Newton and Darwin help us to *"understand the anti-Hellenic world"* we live in. In 1985, the dialogue between the "two cultures" was made official by the Society for Literature and Science, whose publications continue to reflect academic concerns. In "From Science to Literature" (1984),[7] Roland Barthes outlined the similarities between Literature and the various sciences, referring to them as Human and Social Sciences, and demonstrates how the use of language separates them. According to him, scientific discourse adopts an ideal, monolithic voice: one word, one meaning. Science believes that language has a purely instrumental function, whose primary values are clarity and non-ambiguity. Barthes ironizes this belief in a "slave language that is humble and obedient to its demands."

Banville's tetralogy is not based on science, nor is it a fictional rewriting of the scientists' lives. He explores the nature of the scientists' creative processes in order to comprehend his own behaviour in the field of fiction and to do so he does not need to write about artists, as he once said in an interview:

> Yet although the characters in the novels were men who transformed science: they are an attempt to explore the nature of the creative process 'without writing about artists.' His real theme is not the apparent story but fiction itself and the connection between language and experience.[8]

---

[5] Aldous Huxley, *Literature and Science*. New Haven, Leete's Island Books, 1963.
[6] Matthew Arnold, "Literature and Science". In: *Discourses in America* (lecture 2), 1883-1884. pp.15-23.
[7] Roland Barthes, "From Science to Literature". In: *The Rustle of Language*.
[8] Ciaran Carty, "Out of Chaos Comes Order". In The Sunday Tribune. 14 September 1986, p.18.

History and fiction are human constructions, signified systems. The truth is the past perceived by us through documents, oral reports and writings. It is an "archeologized" past as defined by Lemaire.[9] However, when this historical knowledge is questioned and explored in the 'real' past, "literary genres" turn into a *"historiographic metafiction"*, as Linda Hutcheon argues in *The Poetics of Postmodernism*.[10] She appropriates Gottschalk's definition of historiography as the imaginary reconstruction of the process of critical analysis of those events that have survived from the past. I prefer to refer to the tetralogy as a *trans(ap)parent historiographic metabiofiction*, where the past is seen from the present and the limits of biography and fiction are blurred, provoking a tension in the narrative: the biography is articulated as a self-conscious and reflective fiction, transforming the pseudo-historical novel into a *metabiofiction*, and the *transparent*, true facts into *apparent* reality due to the relativity of perception. For Hutcheon, crossing frontiers is a postmodern fictional device. Banville's proposal of a "new synthesis" is transparent, visible and *apparent* at the same time, creating another "supreme fiction", which is equal to the model taken from the past and, in its turn, transcended.

In 1986, Banville declared to Lavinia Greacen that he was writing a historical novel nearly by mistake:

> I didn't know what I had let myself in for, because I blundered in blindly. I really had no interest in catching the grand sweep of the age. I did get annoyed having to do the research, but writing about the distant past you have to do so much and then not use it. It mustn't be seen, otherwise it weighs down and deadens your book, but you have to have done it. You're actually building a basis to work for.[11]

This was reinforced in his interview of April 15th, 1992, in which he said to me that it was not his intention to write historical novels:

---

[9]In: Linda Hutcheon, *The Poetics of Postmodernism*. p.105.
[10]*Ibid.*, pp.105-106.
[11]Lavinia Greacen, "A serious Writer". In: *The Irish Times*, Tuesday, March 24, 1981. p.8

> It was a waste of time and effort. I should not have done that but, at the same time, I do not regret what I did. I should have written that self-questioning without having to read so much. Of course I was looking for the implications of the scientific discoveries, conceptual changes, ways in which the mind of the scientist works.

Although this declaration partly confirms the first one, it reveals his conviction of the correlation between the formation of concepts in "the two cultures". Banville "fictionalises" biographical data concerning the scientists' deconstruction of the processes of their theories and narratives in order to show how scientists' minds work in the formulation of a synthesis and how uncertainties and context also govern the form in which their knowledge is published. *"For the scientist, the significance of indeterminacy will consist in the nature of the limitations it imposes. For the artist, the interest will be esthetic".*[12]

Banville rewrites the processes of the scientific revolutions and demonstrates that knowledge is a construction of the scientist's mind. He tries to explain in a deductive or inductive way the *a priori* or *a posteriori* theories created in his own mind concerning facts perceived sensorially, because the mind can only grasp the laws relating to a phenomenon and not its essence. In line with Copernicus's and Kepler's theories, Banville is interested in this idea, in the order of facts rather than in their definition, as their essence can not be comprehended. Both scientific and fictional "truth" are demonstrated through a metaphorical discourse in the first two books of the tetralogy. Banville questions both what Umberto Eco calls epistemological metaphors - *"the sun rises", "the sun sets"* - false affirmations that describe natural phenomena, and also the significance of fiction itself. The "truths" defended by Astronomy and Physics, History and Fiction, lose their state of probability, becoming predictable in the light of Newton's mechanicist theory. But in *The Newton Letter*, the absolute truths upon which the scientist based his theory come into conflict when influenced by their social context and, later on, they are relativized in *Mefisto*.

The scientific syntheses are transferred analogically to the universe of fiction. There is a mapping of discourses through form to reveal the relationship between language and experience, and the impossibility of the former being a faithful copy of reality: essence is only revealed by an intuitive "flash" and is transformed into "relative" knowledge "mediated" by form. According to Banville, in a Heideggerian sense, the 'intuitive" form of a work of art exists before and after a book is written, becoming a *"sine qua non"* condition of the work of the artist. In *Kepler*, Banville exalts form, the determining element of any true work of art. The writer appropriates Kepler's motto, *"In the beginning is the shape"*, to question, especially in the last book of the tetralogy, *Mefisto*, whether chaos springs from form or is part of it.

The analysis which follows shows that it is through narrative and form that the discourses of science and fiction meet in the field of concepts, in the primacy of imagination and intuition during the process of creation, in the power of persuasion, in the presence of the subjective constituent, in self-referentiality, in the power of metaphor, in the tensions provoked by the social, economic and ideological context, in the formation of knowledge and in its publication.

---

[12] John Banville, "Physics and Fiction: Order from Chaos". In: *The New York Times Book Review*, April 21, 1985. p.42.

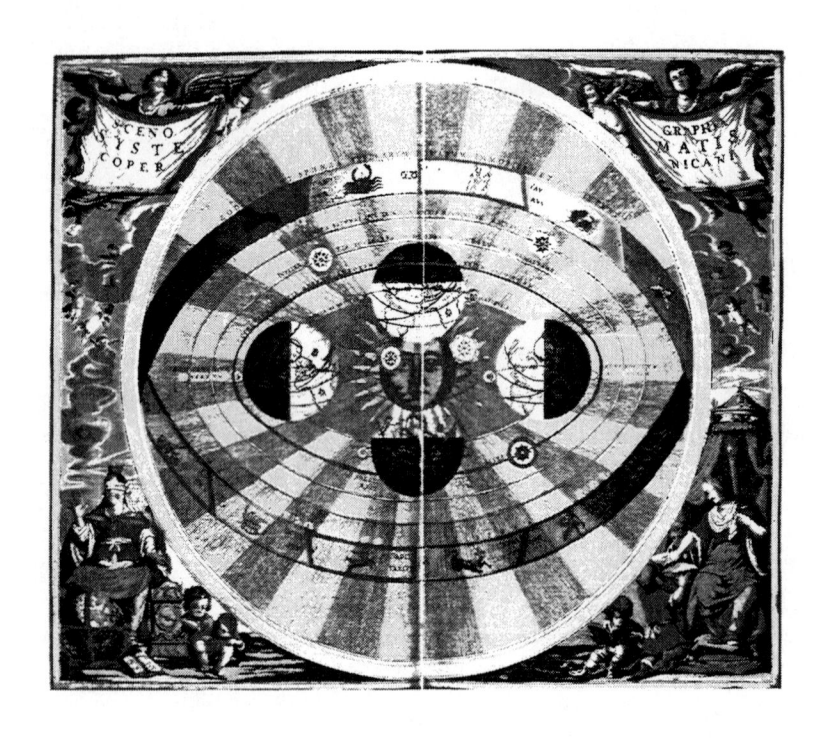

The Copernican System.

Andreas Cellarius, *Atlas Coelestis seu Harmonia Macrocosmica* (Amsterdam, 1660).

Copperplate engraving on paper, hand colored.

Published by Pomegranate Publications, Petaluma, CA. The British Library, London, 1990

(In)Validating *Phenomena* and Fiction

> . . . the birth of the new science must be preceded by a radical act of creation. Out of nothing, next to nothing, disjointed bits and scraps, he would have to weld together an explanation of the phenomena. The enormity of the problem terrified him, yet he knew that it was that problem and nothing less that he had to solve, for his intuition told him so, and he trusted his intuition - he must, since it was all he had. (*Doctor Copernicus*, p. 95)[13]

In *Doctor Copernicus* the technical fallacy of the scientific tradition that validates the inexistant to "save the phenomenon" is revealed. The narrator shows how the Copernican system is constructed and gives birth to a new science that *"would be objective, open-minded, above all honest"*, yet which is preceded by a *"radical act of creation"* based on intuition.[14]

Copernicus, a conservative scientist who is respectful of the tradition expressed in ancestral theories, especially those of Aristotle, questions Ptolemy's geocentric system because the planets do not share a uniform speed and move in a perfect circle as tradition requires. But it is precisely by validating the improbable hypotheses that "save" certain natural phenomena that Copernicus ends up by invalidating that tradition, introducing the heliocentric system which, upon the publication of his book on his death bed, is in reality a vacuum centre system, revealing that, at the centre of everything there is nothing, *"that the world turns upon chaos"*.[15]

Banville is far less concerned with historical facts than with fiction and with the relationship between subject and experience. According to him, the reading of a novel is the most extraordinary process of discovery hinging upon the fascination

---

[13] Quotations refer to the following edition: Banville, John. (1976) *Doctor Copernicus*. London, Panther Books, 1984
[14] *Ibid.* pp.94-95.
[15] Ibid. p. 230

of the gap between what could be real and what is invented, sometimes turning what is more truthful into falsity. For this reason he reconstructs aesthetically the creative process of the scientist based on various biographical and scientific books, though he gives most credit to Thomas Kuhn's *The Copernican Revolution* and Arthur Koestler's *The Sleepwalkers: A History of Man's Changing Vision of the Universe*. As an Irish writer he transforms the scientific, philosophic and socio-fictional narrative discourses into an aesthetic discourse and uses the narrative strategies and form of the scientists themselves in the construction of another fiction in the search for a signifying synthesis of his own: a literary synthesis.

Copernicus opens with the scientist's childhood: his mother's death, later his father's, the separation of his brother Andreas and himself from their sisters and how they were placed under the care of his uncle Canon Lucas, later to become Bishop of Ermland. Certain elements in the scientist's life as narrated in the first part, "Orbitas Lumenque", reveal his solitary character, inquisitive mind and obsession with perfecting a theory inspired by an initial intuition: his interest in Mathematics, his religious career dictated by his uncle, his university studies in Cracow and Italy culminating in his graduation as a Doctor in Canon Law, his belief in the Sun as the centre of the universe and the harmonic movement of the Earth and the other planets around it.

The process of Copernicus's development as a scientist blends with the process of scientific investigation. In the second part, "Magister Ludi", many events are seen as causing the scientist's ostracism and self-imposed silence: Andreas's physical and moral decay, his reluctance to publish his theories, the discrimination suffered since he was a child, initially for being a merchant's son and subsequently as a result of gossip about his having a distant cousin as a housekeeper and concubine, the publication of his theory in *Commentariolus* for a restricted public, and his loss of faith in his theory and the scientific and political power implicit in it.

In the third part, "Cantus Mundi", there is a dislocation of the narrative focus. The sour voice of Rheticus, Copernicus's disciple, narrates in autobiographical form how he summarized and published his master's manuscript and, together with Canon Giese, persuaded him to publish his complete book at the end of his life, in which there is no acknowledgement of his disciple's work. "Magnum Miraculum", the last part of the novel, portrays the death of the scientist with impressionistic strokes. The focus of the narrative changes with every scene, each of which is constructed like a painting: the conviction that death will reveal to him the ultimate truth, an involuntary reflection upon his relationship with Anna, and the visit of Osiander who was responsible for printing his book in Nuremberg. Each picture shows, in first and third person narration, his inner struggle and the balance of life before death.

Banville shows in his narrative how Copernicus's blind faith in Aristotle's principles made him construct a fiction which was partly true and partly fictional: whilst it was true that the earth was really in motion, being the centre of the moon's orbit, and that the sun the centre of the universe, the movement of the planets as it was described in his theory, a system of epicycles similar to Ptolemy's theory, was a geometric fiction. According to Koestler, Copernicus manipulated the orbits of the planets at his will, unable to contest on his death bed Osiander's preface to his book *De revolutionibus orbium mundi*, in which he justified the publication as being no more than another hypothesis seeking to represent natural phenomena exactly, and compared it with previous hypotheses. Banville appropriates Koestler's affirmation from *The Sleepwalkers*, in order to validate not only the role of a fictional construction in the field of science but also to sublimate it in the literary field when dealing with the controversial representation of reality:

> He ceased to believe also in his book. For a while, in Cracow, in Italy, he had succeeded in convincing himself that (what was it?) the physical world was amenable to physical investigation, that the principal thing itself could be said. That faith too had collapsed. The book by now had gone through two complete revisions, rewritings really, but instead of coming nearer to essentials it was, he knew, flying off in a wild eccentric orbit into emptiness; instead of approaching the word, the crucial Word, it was careering headlong into a loquacious silence. He had believed it possible to say the truth; now he saw that all that could be said was the saying. His book was not about the world, but about itself.(*D.C.*, p.128)

This quotation focuses on three fundamental aspects: metafiction in the scientific narrative showing how the book becomes self-contained; the crisis of language in the field of representation; and the epistemological questioning of truth.

Imhof and McMinn both stress the importance of the theme of language in *Doctor Copernicus*. McMinn goes deeper, saying that the tragedy is both personal and intellectual because it is impossible to separate means from ends, and pointing out that it concludes with a painful irony when Copernicus perceives that his theory is no more than an *"exalted naming"*.[16] According to the Irish critic, *"Banville's version of this tragedy adds the vital dimension of language as both means and obstacle to knowledge and perception."* [17] In Rheticus's voice the deception acquires a human dimension:

---
[16] Joseph McMinn, *John Banville. A Critical Study*. p.52.
[17] *Ibid.*, p.53

'Ach, Rheticus!' It was the first time he had called me by that name. 'You do not understand me! You do not understand yourself. You think that to see is to perceive, but listen, listen: seeing is not perception! Why will you not realize that? (...) But do you not understand that, without perception, all these theories are equal in value? Stars or torches, it is all one, all merely an exalted naming; those lights shine on, indifferent to what we call them. My book is not science - it is a dream. I am not even sure if science is possible.' (*D.C.*, p.220)

I believe that the tragedy transcends the personal and intellectual levels that McMinn refers to, achieving also the metafictional level established by the very use of the words. Banville re-reads the sixteenth-century concept of language, portraying the investigations of the scientist from a Wittgensteinean perspective.

According to Foucault in *Les mots et les choses,* similitude helped to construct Western culture in the sixteenth century when representation appeared as repetition. At the same time the semantic texture of similitude was very rich and the fictional Copernicus is depicted as subjecting his ideas to common sense, convenience, emulation, analogy and assimilation. Banville thus explores different notions of similitude in Copernicus's investigations to reveal how the discovery that things are not reflected in language like a mirror provokes a crisis in the scientist's mind. In so doing he reaffirms the existence of a void between the word and what it defines in science as well as in fiction. This may be seen in Rheticus's fictional autobiography, "Cantus Mundi":

> I said:
> *'I hold it true that pure thought can grasp reality, as the ancients dreamed.'*
> He said:
> *'Science aims at constructing a world which shall be symbolic of the world of commonplace experience.'*
> I said:

> *'If you would know the reality of nature, you must destroy the appearance, and the farther you go beyond the appearance, the nearer you will be to the essence.'*
> He said:
> *'It is of the highest significance that the outer world represents something independent of us and absolute with which we are confronted.'* (*D.C.*, p. 221)

The crisis of the word had already been discussed by Banville in *Nightspawn* and *Birchwood*, the latter concluding with Wittgenstein's words *"whereof I cannot speak, thereof I must be silent"*. For the philosopher, the meaning of a word is given by its use. When words are used to refer to objects in the world we are operating within a language game and our concept of "the world" is already conditioned by the structure of the language.[18]

Doctor Copernicus returns to the question raised at the end of *Birchwood* and starts with the Joycean style of *A Portrait of the Artist as a Young Man*, echoing the Book of Genesis in reverse:

> At first it had no name. It was the thing itself, the vivid thing.
> (...) Everything had a name, but although every name was nothing without the thing named, the thing cared nothing for its name, had no need of a name, and was itself only. And then there were the names that signified no substantial thing, as linden and tree signified that dark dancer. (*D.C.*, p.13)

In the chapter entitled "A Crisis of Fiction" in his book *Transitions*,[19] Richard Kearney says that Banville points out the following dilemma: how can the observer know reality if the very words and concepts that define it are means to transform that same reality creatively? If all theories are names and the world is an object, how can the scientist overcome the gap between name and thing?

---

[18] Bryan Magee, *The Great Philosophers.* p.332
[19] Richard Kearney, In: *Transitions. Narratives in Modern Irish Culture.* p.93.

Joseph McMinn observes that if the world comes first, before the word that names it, language will become a *"revitalised means of knowledge."* [20]

The fictitious Copernicus faces the prejudice that tradition cannot be questioned and claims that facts can be explained when he is at an academic meeting at the mathematician and astronomer Professor Adalbert Brudzewski's home in Cracow:

> 'Ptolemy,s theory saves the phenomena, I have said so already; what other responsibility should it have?'
> Tell him. *Tell him.*
> 'Knowledge, *magister*, must become perception. The only acceptable theory is that one which *explains* the phenomena, . . . ' (*D.C.*, p.47)

Copernicus believes that the physical world, reality, could be investigated and explained because astronomers did not describe the world as it really was, only as they observed it. He is accused of being a nominalist because of his search for explanations:

> I a nominalist - I? Do you not merely say the name of Ptolemy and imagine that all contrary arguments are thus refuted? No, no, *magister*, I believe not in names, but in things. (*D.C.*, p.46)

Copernicus's political position becomes public when he reveals the polemic gap between word and object. Rüdiger Imhof associates the language theme with the epistemological search for truth, *"the thing itself."* On his death bed, the fictitious Copernicus is visited by the angel of redemption, personified as the ghost of his dead brother Andreas. Using the narrative technique of *stream of consciousness*, the angel shows him that truth is inside each person, in the world itself, in all things, and he makes him recognise his failure in trying to grasp transcendental truth while he was still attached to language:

---

[20] Joseph McMinn, *John Banville. A Critical Study.* p.67.

- Your soul? Ah, but you did sell it, to the highest bidder. What shall we call it? science? the quest for truth? transcendent knowledge? Vanity, all vanity, and something more, a kind of cowardice, the cowardice that comes from the refusal to accept that the names are all there is that matter, the cowardice that is true and irredeemable despair. With great courage and great effort you might have succeeded, . . . But you tried to discard the commonplace truths for the transcendent ideas, and so failed.(*D.C.*, p.252)

Canon Wodka calms young Copernicus down during his school years when he was in his search for principles to believe in. He explains to him the separation between words and things saying that theories are only names, *"but the world itself is a thing"*.[21]

Influenced by Wittgenstein's thought, Banville portrays a divided Copernicus: he is defending a tradition which he simultaneously counter-attacks. His idea of the universe was based upon *a priori* reasoning. Astronomy is a science of observation rather than experimentation, so the scientist was aware that, although science itself conspires to "save the phenomena", everything was false. The only truth was its negation, that is to say, the truth was false: *"The Ptolemaic astronomy is nothing, so far as existence is concerned, but it is convenient for computing the inexistent"* (198).

Science is a form of ritual or play-acting that tries to transform the chaos of the world into order. If, to attain this, a creative act is necessary, then science resembles art. According to Banville, fiction invents order. Through it he *"creates sense from the chaos of the real world"*.[22] However, the aim of art is not to save the phenomena but *"to lose them, or risk losing them."*[23] I believe that Banville follows the scientist's process of negation analogically, rebelling against the

---

[21] John Banville, *Doctor Copernicus*. p.33.
[22] Ciaran Carty, "Out of Chaos Comes Order". In: *The Sunday Tribune*. 14 Sep. 1986, pp.18-19.
[23] Ronan Sheehan, "Novelists on the Novel". In: *The Crane Bag*. III, 1(1979),. p.79.

tradition which sees language as a transparent and absolute sign of the things because of its similitude:

> . . . surely they (poets and novelists) should be pushing language to its limits, for it is only by risk that language lives fully, constantly renewing itself in the face of challenge. The writer must press down hard on every line, with such force and passion and attentiveness that the words begin to glow, to blush, in the sudden light of self-awareness. This is a dangerous way to write (especially if one is writing in Hiberno-English), but it is better to be drunk on words than sober in the safety of a grey style.[24]

Banville skilfully represents Wittgenstein's fight, first, against his earlier theory that words obtain their meanings when they stand for objects, secondly against the older theory that words acquire their meanings through being associated with ideas in the mind and, finally, against the theory that, for a word to have a meaning, there must be an essence which that word expresses.

> 'We think only those thoughts that we have the words to express, but we acknowledge that limitation only by our wilfully foolish contention that the words mean more than they say; it is a pretty piece of sleight of hand, that: it sustains our illusions wonderfully, until, that is, the time arrives when the sands have run out, and the truth breaks in upon us. Our lives -' he smiled '- are a little journey through God's guts...' (*D.C.*, p. 220)

In Rheticus's narrative, Copernicus blames his disciple for imagining his book to be a mirror that reflects the real world. To construct this mirror the scientist needs to perceive the world in its totality and essence, something that life's disorder does not let him to do. He explains that an illusory mirror is constructed in front of the chaos that appears to reflect the real world, but it merely reflects appearances because chaos is behind it. Here, Rheticus's narrative becomes vehement and accusatory, showing that Copernicus's theory presents a system

---

[24] John Banville, *Weekend Guardian*, July 7-8, 1990. p.20

that tries above all to "save the phenomena", and yet which is all a lie because it broke the mirror and gave way to chaos:

> O, the phenomena were saved, indeed - but at what cost! For in his calculations, not 34 epicycles were required to account for the entire structure of the universe, as the Commentariolus claimed, but 48 - which is 8 more at least than Ptolemy had employed! This little trick, however, is nothing, a mere somersault, compared with the one which I am now about to speak. You imagine that Koppernigk set the Sun at the centre of the universe, don't you? He did not. The centre of the universe according to his theory is not the Sun, but the centre of the Earth's orbit, which, as the great, the mighty, the all-explaining Book of Revolutions admits, is situated at a point in space some three times the Sun's diameter distant from the Sun! All the hypotheses, all the calculations, the star tables, charts and diagrams, the entire ragbag of lies and half truths and self-deceptions which is De revolutionibus orbium mundi (or coelestium, as I suppose I must call it now), was assembled simply in order to prove that at the centre of all there is nothing, that the world turns upon chaos.
> Are you stirring in your grave, Koppernigk? Are you writhing in cold clay? . . . You were evil, Koppernigk, and you filled the world with despair. (*D.C.*, p.230)

In this long passage it may be observed how Banville uses the critic evaluations made by Koestler and Kuhn of Copernicus's scientific concepts, and subverts them in the voice of Rheticus, who is upset at not having had his name publicly acknowledged.

However, Banville does not only exploit the relationship between language and reality from an epistemological perspective, but he also shows how political convenience influences scientific narrative, validating fictional "truth" once more: historically, Osiander explained in his preface that he had changed the title of Copernicus's book, substituting the word *coelestium* for *mundi*, because he thought that it was more convenient to speak about the heavens than about the world in order to establish a wider distance and detachment from the beliefs of the time and the political power of the church. This was the reason that he diminished the value of Copernicus's theory, reducing it to one more hypothesis and describing the scientist as an artist.[25] Banville transforms passages of the Osiander's preface, which was previously thought to have been written by Copernicus himself, and creates a fictitious dialogue between Osiander and Copernicus showing the power relationship through the inner voice of the scientist. He also re-reads Koestler's and Kuhn's research and presents us with a scientist whose theory was manipulated politically by his editor:

> 'I have **altered** the title,' **he said absently,**'as I **may have informed** you was my intention, substituting the word coelestium for mundi, as it **seemed to me safer** to speak of the heavens, thereby displaying distance and **detachment**, rather than of the world, an altogether more immediate term.'
> No, my friend, you did not mention that, as I recall; but it is no matter now.
> 'Also, **of course**, I have **attached** a preface, as **we agreed**. It was **a wise move**, I believe. As I have said to you in my various letters, the Aristotelians and thelogians will easily be placated if **they are told** that **several hypotheses** can be used to explain the **same apparent** motions, and that the **present hypotheses** are not proposed because they are in reality true, but because they are the **most convenient** to calculate the apparent composite motions'. (...) 'For my part,' the Lutheran went on, 'I have always felt about hypotheses and they are not articles of faith, but bases of computation, so that even **if they are false** it does not matter, **provided that they save** the phenomena ... And in the light of this belief have I composed the preface.'
> 'It must not be,' the Canon said, his dull gaze turned upward towards the ceiling. Osiander stared at him.
> 'What?'
> 'It must not be: I do not wish the book to be published.'
> 'But...it is already published, my dear sir. (...)' (*D.C.*, p.246)

The words and phrases I have emphasised here in bold are charged with strong ideological connotations. Copernicus wanted to cancel publication and collect in

---

[25]Part of the original text was published in "To the Reader Concerning the Hypotheses of this Work". In: *Great Books of the Western World. No.16 Ptolemy, Copernicus, Kepler.* pp.505-506.

the distributed copies because he had failed to discern the truth - *"the significance of things"*. However, death prevented him from finishing his act.

Banville explores the idea that political manipulations are also responsible for the production of fictions in both fields, the scientific and the political. To portray this influence, he chooses the historical moment that Poland declared war on Prussia and the Frauenberg Chapter decided to intervene to reconcile the parties. Precentor Giese and Canon Koppernigk meet Lutheran Grand Master Albrecht at a peace conference and, when Copernicus asks Albrecht to consider the suffering that war with Poland would bring the people, he reveals:

> 'You and I, *mein Freund*, we are lords of the earth, the great ones, the major men, the makers of supreme fictions. (...) The people - peasants, soldiers, generals - they are my tool, as mathematics is yours, by which I come directly at the true, the eternal, the real. Ah yes, Doctor Copernicus, you and I - you and I!' (*D.C.*, p.149)

This crude "truth" makes Copernicus lose his faith in science and opt for silence, concentrating on his everyday religious obligations, dedicating himself obsessively to curing the poor and establishing the mathematical formulae to explain his scientific hypotheses.

The influence of the political context on the fictional narrative was already present in the first novels, but *Doctor Copernicus* deals with the political question from a metafictional point of view, referring to the essence of the art of writing and its power when the two characters, the fictional and the historical, are reflected through the principle of similitude called emulation. According to Foucault, the emulation principle is partially similar to the reflection in a mirror. Through it, things spread in the world, corresponding to each other. Emulation is born from a division of the self, in which both sides confront each other. Foucault associates this concept with Paracelsus when he compares this duplication with the image of twins who resemble each other, although it is impossible to say who gives the other their similitude.[26] This image is ubiquitous in Banville's work, inserted in the presence of the other as a ghost that afflicts the main character, as in *Nightspawn*, or as in the opposite twin in *Birchwood*. In *Copernicus*, Andreas is the other, the reverse side of the coin: determined to live life as it is, he torments the scientist, who refuses to live the same experience because of his search for a "transcendental truth".

This emulation in the construction of his characters is repeated in the construction of the narrative where he seeks the essence of fiction and the political power of questioning art. I have shown how the political context obliged Osiander to write a preface to the reader in order to prevent reactionary attitudes against the scientist and his theory. Historically, Copernicus also wrote a preface and a dedication to Pope Paul III justifying his conclusions. He says that his results arose from the uncertainty present in the formulae of traditional Mathematics, in the questions of the philosophers that pointed to the probability of a heliocentric system and, above all, in deference to the request of his friends - the Cardinal of Capua, the Bishop of Kulm (Tiedeman Giese) and the Bishop of Fossombrone - to improve the Ecclesiastical Calendar, something which Leo X had postponed due to the lack of correct data concerning the duration of the year and months and the solar and lunar movements. His preface was thus clearly written in an attempt to canvass the political support of the Church.[27]

---

[26] Michael Foucault, *Les mots et les choses*. Trans. *As palavras e as coisas*. pp.35-36.
[27] "Preface and Dedication to Pope Paul III". In: *Great Books of the Western World. No.16 Ptolemy, Copernicus, Kepler*. pp.509.

In his youth, Rheticus rebelled against the political conveniences of the time, above all when his work was not recognised due to his Lutheran faith: *"He was not thinking of me, but of the consequences of me, so to speak (What will the Bishop say!)"* (178). According to him, Copernicus, who *"had represented . . . the very spirit incarnate of the New Age"*, became a cautious *"cold old brute"* only worried about appearances and the security of his prebend; he was afraid of the people who would not understand his theory.

Banville's work is self-referential and he constantly shows the crisis of the word in relation to things echoing Wittgenstein's voice in an ironic way, and the political influence of the context. These themes were to be revisited in his subsequent novels. In *Kepler,* the scientist writes to master Mästlin during the political confusion of his country and the religious persecution:

> *I do not speak like I write, I do not write like I think, I do not think like I ought to think, and so everything goes on in deepest darkness.* Where did these voices come from, these strange sayings? It was as if the future had found utterance in him." (*K.*, p.85).[28]

In *The Newton Letter*, Banville's historian narrator opens the novel writing *"Words fail me, Clio."*[29]

Banville's tetralogy validates the questioning of representations in the field of science. He starts with the revealing process of how Copernicus stops believing in truth because it is no more than a construction of the mind expressed through imprecise language. Rheticus's subversive discourse in "Cantus Mundi" reaffirms the presence of *"pathetic fictions"* on the threshold of the New Age in the scientific world, arguing that those who would like to be in the game should

---
[28] All the quotations refer to this edition: Banville, John. *Kepler,*.London, Panther Books, 1985.
[29] John Banville, *The Newton Letter*. London: Panther Books, 1984. p.9. (Quotations hereafter refer to this edition).

accept them.[30] The theme in *Kepler* is developed with an interrogative attitude of uncertainty in relation to science as a game and to the magic of numbers, which have a mysticism that has to be subverted. Historical truth is checkmated in *The Newton Letter* where absolute truths turn into relative truths, and *Mefisto* is based on an existentialist investigation of chaos.

The chain of scientific enunciations is transformed into "convenient" discourses, which conspire with the narrative form chosen by the author to reveal a constructed "truth". This process also resembles the way in which the novelist appropriates contemporary or past social practices to reveal a "reality" that is reconstructed through the word, through the aesthetic fictional form.

The Convenient Form

> Begin, ephebe, by perceiving the idea
> Of this invention, this invented world,
> The inconceivable idea of the sun.
>
> You must become an ignorant man again
> And see the sun again with an ignorant eye
> And see it clearly in the idea of it.
> W. Stevens,
> in: "Notes Toward a Supreme Fiction"

There can be no doubt that Wallace Stevens's poem is Banville's source of inspiration for his tetralogy on the scientists. He uses the second stanza of "It Must Be Abstract" as an epigraph of *Doctor Copernicus*. Here, the epigraph contains the first and second stanzas of the poem to introduce the author's belief in the power of perception and invention in the construction of reality, a theme that was to be developed further in *Kepler*.

---

[30] John Banville, *Doctor Copernicus*, p.172.

The first book of the tetralogy proves that, where science depends on fictitious expression, the *differance* explored by Banville through his fictional narrative is shown in the way both scientist and artist construct a fiction as an attempt to "explain" and not to "save" appearances. The exaltation of form was to occur in the next novel, *Kepler*, an immanent semiotic system, in which the pluralism and hybridity of the postmodern narrative are demonstrated.

The starting point for Banville's books is shape. Though he affirms that it is not a geometric shape but *"a sort of tension in the vacuum"*,[31] *Doctor Copernicus* and *Kepler* go beyond the narrative forms that the very scientists used when they made their theories public. The geometric shape appears either in the narrative or in the construction of the novel, as happens mainly in *Kepler*, whose chapters reproduce regular geometric forms while the narrative is either circular or elliptical according to the argument defended by the scientist, as will be demonstrated later.

Copernicus (1473-1543) published the basic principles of his theory in his manuscript *Commentariolus* (1530). He distributed a few copies among those scholars he considered to be discreet and sympathetic to his hypotheses, due to the controversy his theory might generate. The first two parts of Banville's book, *Orbitas Lumenque* and most of *Magister Ludi*, are third person narrations. The language used is "objective-descriptive", informative, with a tone of detachment as if it were not only a scientific narrative, but also historical. However, there is a dramatic narrative in the dialogues of the characters where fictional creativity confirms Banville's assumption that novelists are *"for imagining things more vividly than historians can ever do"*.[32] At the end of the second part, the narrative is in the epistolary form where the importance of the scientist's work is overshadowed by his personal life because he is accused by the church of having a *focaria* - Anna Schillings. In these letters the aim is to give the appearance of personal life, which represents analogically the investigations into the appearance

---
[31] Ciaran Carty, "Out of Chaos Comes Order". In: The Sunday Tribune, 14 Sep., 1986. pp.18-19.

of the natural phenomena, transforming the fictional space into a Foucauldean doubt on certainties.

Kuhn's scientific analysis in the chapter "Copernicus' innovation", uses the example of the monster that Copernicus describes in his preface to Pope Paul III, in his book *De Revolutionibus Orbium Mundi*. He refers to a picture by an artist which represents a human body made up of the sum of the best drawings of its parts, belonging not to a single man but to different models. Copernicus likens this monstrous form to the form of the Universe, deduced from the sum of wrong mathematical data and formulae. Kuhn concludes that the two most important characteristics of this Copernican monster are dispersion and error, which generate discontentment due to the element of uncertainty in the search for the "real". Just as Copernicus departs from an analogy with painting to demonstrate scientifically a wrong conception of the world, Banville inserts scientific concepts into his aesthetic discourse. The permanent doubt present in any questioning or scientific solution permeates the fictional and epistolary narratives present in the book, similarly generating uncertainty about the relationship between the scientist and his *focaria*, as seen mainly through the correspondence between the Bishops of Ermland and Kulm.

The Bishop of Ermland, Johannes Dantiscus, wrote to the Bishop of Kulm and Copernicus's friend, Tiedemann Giese, telling him of his suspicion about Copernicus's affair with Anna Schillings, *"It is suggested that he keeps her as his focaria, & that she fulfils all duties attaching to such a position, being housekeeper & also concubine"* (164). Giese answered that the Canon had already dismissed Anna and had not seen her any more, adding that he deserved credibility and respect due to his advanced age and infinite dedication to his studies. But Rheticus's narrative reveals that, although Copernicus had tried to get free of her, he was strongly subject to her will. Rheticus manipulates speculative

---

[32]*Ibid.*

science as his master and concludes by speculating on their relationship because he is the witness of an appearance:

> I confess it made me feel quite nauseous to ponder the matter, but I surmised that some cuntish ritual, performed years before when they were still capable of that kind of thing, had subjected him to her will. I have seen it before, that phenomenon, men turned into slaves by the tyranny of the twat. Women. I have nothing against them, in their place, but I know that they have only to master a few circus tricks in bed and they become veritable Circes. Ach, leave it, Rheticus, leave it. (*D.C.*, p.203)

In the last part, when Copernicus is dying, the narrator refers to that mysterious link and an epiphany deconstructs the Canon's investigation into what Anna had meant to him in his life: *"For the first time it struck him as odd that they had never in all the years learned to call each other **thou**"* (239).

Though the final reflection shows the consummation of the affair, it generates the doubt as to whether this might not have been another creation of the scientist's mind in his agonising death:

> She had been his housekeeper, and, on three occasions, more than that, three strange, now wholly unreal encounters into which he had been led by desperation and unbearable self-knowledge and surrender; she had thrice, then, been more, but not much more, certainly not enough to justify Dantiscus's crass relentless hounding. Now, however, he wondered if perhaps those three nights were due a greater significance than he had been willing to grant. Perhaps, for her, they had been enough to keep her with him. For she could have left him. . . . She had chosen to remain. She had endured. Was this what she signified, what she meant? He recalled green days of hers, storms in spring and autumn moods, grievings in wintertime. He should have shown her more regard, then. Now it was too late. (*D.C.*, p.243)

The letters between Dantiscus, Giese and Copernicus occupy the transitional space between the pseudo-historical and biographical narrative and the beginning of Rheticus pseudo-autobiographical narrative in *Cantus Mundi*. These letters introduce the narrative forms that the historical Rheticus used to make Copernicus's theory known in *Narratio Prima* (1540), which is the summary of the new theory in the epistle form addressed to his former master, and in an unpublished biography of the scientist.

Rheticus's autobiographical narrative reveals the *tour de force* of a mind revolted against its master for not having been acknowledged his Herculean work in the preface to *De Revolutionibus Orbium Caelestium* (1543). Rheticus had copied Copernicus's manuscripts and had made the first contacts for its publication. Osiander assumed the final revision of the text due to the discredit suffered by Rheticus after his involvement with Raphaël, the young boy who had served him while he was copying the manuscript at Löbau Castle where Bishop Giese lived. This part and the last one are the most engaging because they appeal to what Riffaterre calls the rhetorical power of *"fictional truth"*: Banville maximises the linguistic perception to portray his "fictional truth". The historical Rheticus, who wrote the scientist's biography which was never published and was finally lost, gives way to the fictitious Rheticus, who selects for his pseudo-autobiography the worst moments of upset provoked by his master's indifference, and transforms them into a passionate and vengeful report. He starts the narrative as though it were a declaration that affirms an absolute truth which has to be believed in:

> I, Georg Joachim von Luachen, called Rheticus, will now set down the true account of how Copernicus came to reveal to a world wallowing in a stew of ignorance the secret music of the universe.(*D.C.*, p.171)

Thus, the truth questioned by the scientist becomes an absolute certainty in Rheticus's voice and he describes the master's behaviour as the reverse of the theories he preaches: he is concerned about appearances, he does not believe in truth, he does not question tradition, which follows convenient rules in order to compute inexistence, he saves phenomena. Rheticus claims that he knows the truth and is a better astronomer than Copernicus, *"but he possessed one precious thing that I lacked - I mean a reputation"* (218). He claims to have corrected the errors of his master's formulae when Copernicus referred to the fact that the orbits of the planets were elliptical (this speculation appears in the manuscripts of the historical Copernicus):

> So that there was little more for me in this scribbling than aching knuckles, and the occasional, malicious pleasure of correcting his slips (I crossed out that nonsensical line in which he speculated on the possibility of elliptical orbits - *elliptical orbits*, for God's sake!). . . . that the work was all my own. The cretin. (D.C., p.215)

However, Rheticus chooses uncertainty as a narrative device when he narrates his personal affair with Raphaël. This narrative within the narrative is a reproduction of the first one on Copernicus's life and goes beyond it in the use of the personal tone when he shows his raw emotions:

> Raphaël he was called, hardly more than a child, a pretty fellow with an arse on him like a peach. O, I knew what he was about! - Raphaël, indeed, some angel. But I followed him willingly enough, and not without gratitude. (*D.C.*, p.182)

In the last part, the point of view changes alternatively from third person to first person narration, as though the reader is penetrating deeper not only into the mind of the agonising scientist, who is anxious to close the gap between words and things before his death, but also into his human nature when his past becomes present. Banville transposes the "reality" of the historical facts, portraying the fictional Copernicus in the voice of the narrator and, using the stream of consciousness technique, he mirrors the chaos that frightened the scientist so much in his search for truth, order and beauty.

If *Doctor Copernicus* is an example of the convenient form transformed into an aesthetic expression by the writer's literary skill, *Kepler* is the perfect synthesis, the realisation of Banville's theory of the external imposition of form.

A Synthesis Emanating from Form

> ... before I have any clear knowledge of what the contents will be, I have already conceived the form of my projected book. It is ever thus with me: in the beginning is the shape! hence I forsee a work divided into five parts, to correspond to the five planetary intervals, while the number of chapters in each part will be based upon the signifying quantities of each of the five regular or Platonic solids which, according to my Mysterium, may be fitted into these intervals. (John Banville, *Kepler*, p. 145)

The construction of the second novel of the tetralogy is based on Kepler's theory (1571-1630). He claimed that, between the six known planets of the solar system, five regular geometric polygons could be inserted. Kepler's fictional letter written to Von Hohenburg, quoted here in the epigraph, is the sign that points to Banville's theory that shape is imposed by the external world. The writer confirms this in an interview to Rüdiger Imhof:

> Always I begin with the shape. But let me make a distinction, a very important one. The form of, say, Kepler, is in itself wholly synthetic, by which I mean that it is imposed from outside, yet by synthetic I do not mean false, or insincere. It is, this formal imposition, the means by which I attempt to show forth, in the Heideggerian sense, the intuitive shape of the particular work of art which is Kepler, and which was there, inviolate, before and after the book was written. I am aware that this sounds suspiciously like mysticism - or hokum, if you prefer - but once again I can only say that this is the way I work, the way I must work, and that it is sincere, with the peculiar sincerity of art.[33]

In this statement he visualises a synthesis in the art of writing, a synthesis that lies between mysticism, intuition and the empirical act of writing, which resembles analogically the Pythagorean synthesis proposed by the scientist:

---
[33] *IUR.*, pp.6-7.

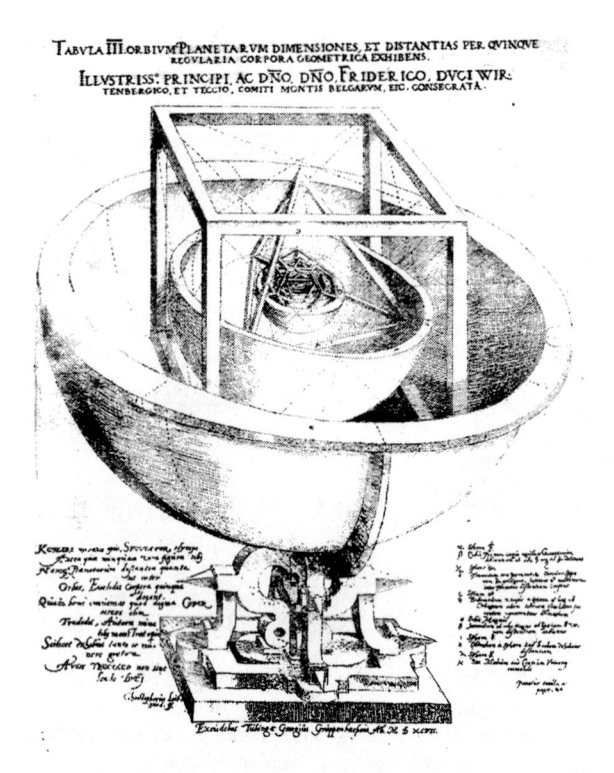

Kepler's *cosmic chalice*

Rare Books and Manuscripts Division. The New York Public Library, Astor, Lenox & Tilden Foundations.

In: *Tempo e Espaço*. Rio de Janeiro: Abril Livros, 1993.

mysticism and science, imagination and reasoning. In his book *Harmonici Mundi*, Kepler was the first and last to attempt to explain the ultimate secret of the universe in an all-embracing synthesis of geometry, music, astrology, astronomy and epistemology. According to Koestler, there is a fragmentation of experience after Kepler, *"science is divorced from religion, religion from art, substance from form, matter from mind."* [34] Banville reinterprets this synthesis in the field of fiction and, like Kepler, he follows the *instinctus divinus* in the construction of his work of art.

The scientist was fascinated by geometric figures and he proposed to Duke Frederic of Württemberg that he should shape the *"cosmic chalice"* in silver mirroring his model of the universe, with the five polygons between the six planets shaped in precious stones. The chalice would contain seven different beverages as Koestler describes quoting Kepler himself. Banville recreates the scientific description aesthetically when the fictitious Kepler explains his idea whilst having supper in the *trippeltisch* in the Duke's castle:

> A young soldier with a moustache, dismembering a piece of chicken, eyed him thoughtfully. 'Seven different kinds of beverage, you say?'
> Johannes ignored the martial manner.
> 'Seven, yes,' he said: 'aqua vitae from the sun, brandy from Mercury, Venus mead, and water from the moon,' busily ticking them off on his fingers, 'Mars a vermouth, Jupiter a white wine, and from Saturn -' he tittered '- from Saturn will come only a bad old wine or beer, so that those ignorant of astronomy may be exposed to ridicule.' (*K*. p.36)

Kepler made two paper models to prove the viability of the project, staying nearly six months in the Duke's court till it was accepted. Banville reproduces the scientist-artist's obsession by means of a "supreme fiction", as Imhof defines it in

---

[34] Arthur Koestler. *The Sleepwalkers*. p.389.

his essay "John Banville's Supreme Fiction",[35] due to the geometrical construction of the book and the structure of its narrative.

Banville constructs *Kepler* in five parts. Each one represents one of the five geometrical figures, which are named after the books published by the scientist: "Mysterium Cosmographicum" (1596), "Astronomia Nova" (1609), "Dioptrice" (1614), "Harmonice Mundi" (1619) and "Somnium" (1634). The textual space and time of each chapter have the same duration and are symmetrical, and the number of the chapters of each part corresponds to the number of the sides of each of the five polygons: there are six chapters in Part I representing the cube embedded in between Saturn and Jupiter; Part II has four chapters, representing the tetrahedron or pyramid placed between Jupiter and Mars; Part III is divided into twelve chapters, relating to the dodecahedron inserted between the spheres of Mars and Earth; Part IV is made up of twenty letters, corresponding to the icosahedron between Earth and Venus; the eight chapters of Part V represent the octahedron placed between the spheres of Venus and Mercury.[36] This division, apparently so technical and contradictory to the generally held concept of beauty, inherent to art, reflects the interest of the time in science as a method of obtaining knowledge through apparent demonstrations and not through the questioning of the origin of that knowledge. As Copernicus observed first, no model needs to be empirically true, only to be plausible and true to the observations upon which it is based, in order to discover the true music of the cosmos and its harmony. Thus, shape is the point of departure that constructed the semiotic meaning of this book. It shows the passage from traditional science to the beginning of modern science, the transition from a science that defended the observation of Nature to another kind of science

---

[35] In: *Irish University Review.* Spring 1981. pp. 52-86
[36] Ibid. pp. 80-84.

that opened the way to its explanation. The need to *explain* the phenomena rises from the master's *a priori* theory and Kepler maximises this, publicly questioning why it is important to show the physical cause of their existence, as he describes the movement of the spheres geometrically. To do this, he needs to attack Copernicus's data for being inexact and unreliable because the scientist used to adapt them to his purpose, as Koestler quotes from Kepler's *Mysterium Cosmographicum*.[37]

In his book *Harmonici Mundi*, the young Kepler defended a unifying truth between God's mind and the human mind because Geometry is co-eternal with the mind of God. Geometry provided God with a model for the Creation and it was *"implanted into man"*.[38] "Divine" Geometry reveals the ultimate eternal truths, it is God himself and it exists before Creation. Thus, he believed that it was possible to deduce the mystery of the universe through *a priori* reasoning, reading the mind of the Creator. Banville recreates an echo of this mysticism in the voice of Kepler as a student, when he discusses the concept of his *idée fixe* with his master Mästlin:

> He felt transparent. There was a whirring high in the air, and then suddenly a crash of bells that made his nerves vibrate. 'Why waste words?' he said, yelled, bells, *damn*. 'Geometry existed before the Creation, is co-eternal with the mind of God, *is God himself* . . .'
> Bang.
> Ó! Mästlin stared at him.
> '...For what,' smoothly, 'exists in God that is not God himself?' (*K*., p.33)

---

[37] Arthur Koestler, *The Sleepwalkers*. p.257.
> *"He selects observations from Ptolemy, Walter and others with a view to making his computations easier, and he does not scruple to neglect or to alter occasional hours in observed time and quarter degrees of angle."*

[38] J. Kepler, *Harmonice Mundi*. In: KOESTLER. *The Sleepwalkers*. p.262.

When the historical Kepler was fifty years old he wrote in the preface to the second edition of *Mysterium Cosmographicum* that he perceived the theory he had formulated when he was twenty-five not as a pure invention of his mind but as something which had been dictated to him as if by a *"heavenly oracle."* [39]

In *The Sleepwalkers*, Koestler mentions that the *a priori* deductions in the first half of *Mysterium* also carried a medieval and mystical tone which seems to be impossible as they belong to one of the founders of modern science. The second half of the book is modern and empirical, and it shows the passage from metaphysical speculation to empirical science. The following books by the scientist were demonstrations of hypotheses raised in the first one, where the *idée fixe* still persists, *"the emanation of the immense emotion that these ideas carry"* as Koestler said, and where the three fundamental laws are presented as by-products of the central idea which, though wrong, is extremely fertile.

In my opinion, Banville takes the scientist's supreme fiction as a model - his *idée fixe* - and he very carefully designs a narrative that has Kepler's three laws as its starting point: the first one refers to the elliptical orbit followed by the planets moving around the Sun which stands at one focus; the second claims that a straight line between the sun and a planet sweeps out equal areas of the ellipse in equal times; and the third postulates that the square of the period of revolution of a planet about the sun is proportional to the cube of the mean distance from the planet to the sun. Thus, in Part I, as Kepler had not postulated the elliptical orbit yet, the period of time of the narrative of "Mysterium Cosmographicum", advances and retrieves symmetrically from one point to the centre returning to the starting point: the number 0.00429. This number is the key that is to unveil the

---

[39]In: Arthur Koestler, *The Sleepwalkers*. p.252.

cosmic mystery which the fictitious Kepler dreams of when he arrives at the palace of Benatek where Tycho Brahe is waiting for him. This consciously uncomprehensible number provides the formula of the ellipsis. The centre of the circular narrative is the questioning of the fact that truth is incidental while harmony is the whole. The advance, retrocession and catalysis of time are achieved through the use of flashbacks and foreshadowings as well as elongations of the present of the narrative. The political and family disorder are part of the chaos that upsets his mind, for example, the deaths of his newly-born sons, the relationship with his first wife, the political changes that result in religious persecution and his own exile. Kepler discovers that Copernicus's mistake was omission and it generates the doubt which guides him in his search for truth:

> Then had Copernicus believed that his system was a picture of reality, or had he been satisfied that it agreed, more or less, with appearances? Or did the question arise? There was no sustained music in that old man's world, only chance airs and fragments, broken harmonies, scribbled cadences. It would be Kepler's task to draw it together, to make it sing. For truth was the missing music.(*K.*, p.29)

Part II is named "Astronomia Nova" and opens with Kepler reconciled with Tycho Brahe and promising to him to solve the problem of the orbit of Mars in seven days. However, this time turns into seven months, seven years and even more. Seven is the number of perfection, of the seven planets known at that time which move in a perfect circle. But what was the truth? In the middle of a disorderly tavern, in which people are dancing and a whore is provoking him, he discovers that the principle of uniform velocity is not valid:

> . . . and all at once out of nowhere, out of everywhere, out of the fiddle music and the flickering light and the pounding of heels, the circling dance and the Italian's drunken eye, there came to him the ragged fragment of a thought. False. What false? That principle. One of the whores was pawing

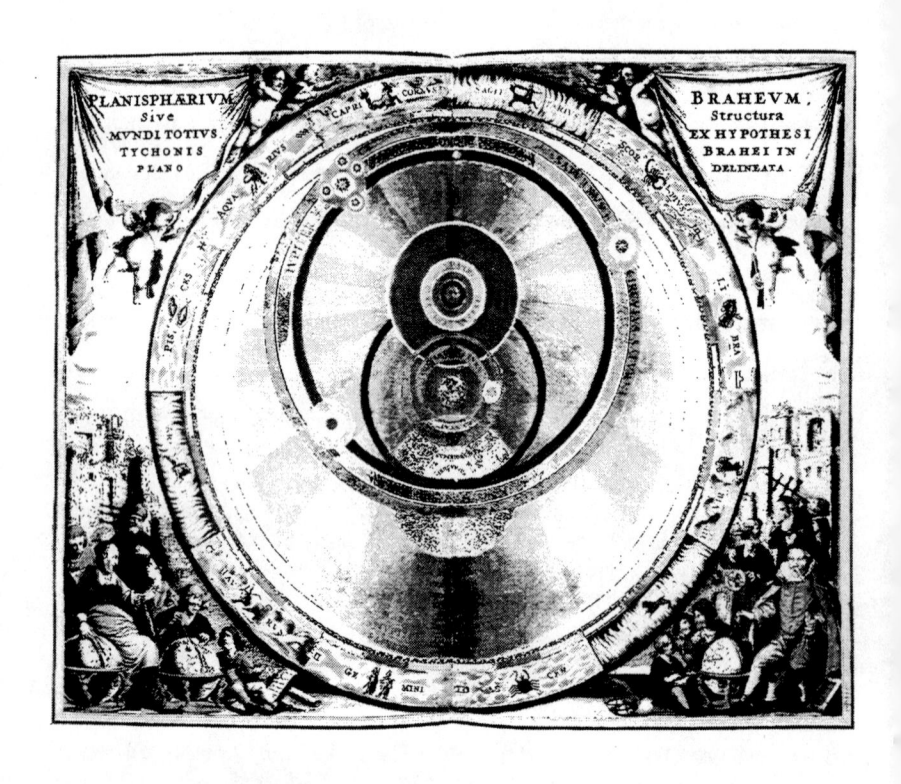

Map of the Universe According to Tycho Brahe's System.
Andreas Cellarius, *Atlas Coelestis seu Harmonia Macrocosmica* (Amsterdam, 1660).
Copperplate engraving on paper, hand colored.
Published by Pomegranate Publications, Petaluma, CA. The British Library, London, 1990

him. Yes, he had it. The principle of uniform velocity is false. He found it very funny, and smiling turned aside and vomited absent-mindedly into a drain. . . . False, by Jesus, yes! (*K.*, p.72)

In this part the narrative, which is divided into four chapters, is characterised by accelerations and decelerations, reproducing the velocity of the planets moving around the sun. Both historical and narrative times are linear. Only the past, the time of memory, returns in the last chapter, when Kepler and Tycho are discussing the project for Tabulae Rudolphinae. There is thus a link with the first chapter and with the acceleration of the planets when they pass near the focus where the sun is to design an elliptical orbit. The narrative is not circular any more, the questioning of an unquestionable truth is the dislocated centre reflecting the new scientific theory. Kepler asks himself what is the validity of a search for another answer when there is already a "correct" one, *"Next he would be claiming that the planets do not move in perfect circles! Kepler shrugged"* (74).

"Dioptrice", the title of the third part, refers to the field of optics that deals with the refraction of light. Atmospheric refraction is the deviation of light reflected by the planets when the rays touch the Earth's atmosphere. This atmospheric refraction deforms various natural phenomena perceived by the human eye. For example, the planets do not appear in their true position; they are seen when they are still below the horizon. Metonymically, "Dioptrice" is a retrogression/ introspection to a past that is deformed or enlightened by the refraction of the light of memory, offering new meanings to the fictional Kepler. His personal life is seen through various lenses, which either deform or sublimate it showing his chaotic relationship with his former wife, the sublimation of Regina, his former wife's daughter from her first marriage, and of his predilection for his son Friedrich, who died when he was six. The flashbacks are like the reflection of the stars, having different degrees of light, inconstantly appearing and disappearing quickly among the clouds of oblivion and the past; they change the colour and brightness of the juxtaposing events according to the relative present. Nevertheless, memories of the esoteric activities of his mother produce "trans(ap)parent" effects in Kepler's fictional present, augmenting or diminishing their importance depending on the degree of chaos present in his personal life. The narrative starts with the reunion of the scientist with his mother and family and ends with his departure. There is an elliptical movement and the dislocated centre that questions life and death is the time of memory going back to his childhood and, even beyond that, to the maternal womb:

> The years were falling away, like loops of rope into a well. Below him there was darkness, an intimation of waters. He might have been an infant himself, now. All at once, like a statue hoving into the window of a moving carriage, Grandfather Sebaldus rose before him, younger and more vigorous than Johannes remembered having known him. There were others, a very gallery of stark still figures looking down on him. Deeper he sank. The water was warm. Then in the incarnadine darkness a great slow pulse began to beat. (*K.*, p.97).

There is a radical change of discourse and point of view in Part IV, "Harmonice Mundi". The epistolary narrative comprises twenty letters written by Kepler, each one occupying the same textual space. According to Imhof, the last ten resemble the image reflected on a mirror, it is a "re-presentation". Time advances in linear fashion, with accelerations and catalyses, from 1605 to 1612, and regresses, again in linear fashion to 1605. The addressees are the same and the dislocated centre appears in the two letters to Röslin in 1609 (the fourth and the seventeenth). The presence of an *instinctus divinus*, a special illumination in the interpretation of the celestial phenomena, is recognized there, validating rhythm, harmony and also disorder. To question nature is to trace geometric relations and this significance is translated with the same symmetry with which the letters were ordered. The change of discourse is related to the difficulty of "trans-posing" ideas using language. The labyrinth of meanings created by the void between the signifier and the signified is revisited by the writer again and again, as in his previous novels.

Part V, "Somnium", resembles Part I because it describes Kepler remembering facts from his past, in a discontinuous and disconnected way, with febrile intensity. The circular narrative shows that memory is the centre that brings to the present a perfect synthesis of his book *Harmonice Mundi*. Here he claims that the perception of harmony is *"instinct in the soul"*:

> The *Harmonia* was their synthesis. . . . Years before, he had defined harmony as that which the soul creates by perceiving how certain proportions in the world correspond to prototypes existing in the soul. The proportions everywhere abound, in music and the movements of the planets, in human and vegetable forms, in men's fortunes even, but they are all relation merely, and inexistent without the perceiving soul. How is such perception possible? Peasants and children, barbarians, animals even, feel harmony of the tone. Therefore the perceiving must be instinct in the soul, based in a profound and essential geometry, that geometry which is derived from the simple divisioning of circles. All that he had for long held to be the case. Now he took the short step to the fusion of symbol and object. The circle is the bearer of pure harmonies, pure harmonies are innate in the soul, and so the soul and the circle are one. (*K.*, p.174)

Harmony is shape, and the circle encloses the purest of the harmonies which are innate to the soul; circle and soul are thus one. The revelation that the world is a more complex construction than he had imagined, makes him aware of the error of having been searching for a perfect and closed cosmos when he was in fact listening to a single melody instead of the various symphonies of which the cosmos is composed:

> A mere clockwork could be nothing beside the reality, which is the most harmonic possible. The regular solids are material, but harmony is form.

> The solids describe the raw masses, harmony prescribes the fine structure, by which the whole becomes that which it is, a perfected work of art. (*K.*, p.176)

Here the fictional Kepler recognizes his thirty-year search for the final synthesis that is represented in *Harmonice Mundi*. The first two books of his masterpiece reveal the harmony in Mathematics, and in the following ones he applies the same concept to Music, Astrology and Astronomy. Banville counterpoints chaos with harmony in the last part of the book. He portrays the political chaos in Prague, the religious persecutions, the scientist's excommunication for having affirmed that the Sacrament of communion was "a symbol", and the judgement of his mother, who had been accused of witchcraft, in contrast with Kepler's personal harmony in his relationship with his second wife. His exhausting journeys in search of the money the Emperor owed him as Mathematician of the Court are also narrated as the publication of Tycho Brahe's *Tabulae Rudolphinae* depended on its payment.

The last book written by the historical Kepler, *Somnium*, which, according to Koestler, was the first work of science fiction in the modern sense, was about his dream-project of a journey to the Moon. Banville uses this book as a model in the construction of a science-fiction-like narrative, where the real blends with the improbable imaginary, and scientific descriptions fuse with disconnected historical facts as though in a dream. The dreams that guided the scientist in his discoveries, reality seen as dreamlike images, his deceptions and actions, and the equilibrium of his life itself are all equally dreamlike. *"It was as in a dream, where it slowly dawns that you are the one who has committed the crime. He knew that these were grossly solipsistic conceits, and yet ... "* (161).

Like Copernicus, the fictional Kepler experiences a final revelation at the end of the novel: just before his death, he discovers the secret of life, the meaning of his dreams, which will never die – *"Never die, never die"* (185).

In the last part, Banville refers to the content of Kepler's book *Somnium*, written twenty years before his death and which he kept as a fragment with some scientific notes which he added sporadically. The book, which was published posthumously, begins with autobiographical allusions and narrates the adventures of a boy called Duracotus who lived with his mother Fiolxhilda in Iceland. Being a witch, she possessed magical powers and conjured up the demons of Lavania to take her son and herself on a journey to the Moon when he arrived after five years of study with Tycho Brahe on an island. The scientist manipulates fantasy and reality, describing the surface of the Moon, its inhabitants, the different forms of life and explaining simultaneously the laws of Physics and the difficulties of breathing due to the velocity of the spaceship. He also postulates the effects of the force of acceleration, the concept of zero gravity zones and comes close to perceiving the universal laws of gravity. Banville stresses the significance of Kepler's book in the denouement of his novel:

> None of his books had given him such peculiar pleasure as this one. It was as if some old strain of longing and love were at last being freed. The story of the boy Duracotus, and his mother Fiolxhilda the witch, and the strange sad stunted creatures of the moon, filled him with quiet inner laughter, at himself, at his science, at the mild foolishness of everything. (*K.*, p.183)

Banville is here referring to Koestler's belief that, since Kepler's work and discoveries were all acts of catharsis, it was appropriate that his last publication should be a fantasy.[40]

"Somnium" is the synthesis that confirms Richard Kearney's critical evaluation of *Kepler*. He argues that Banville juxtaposes the *inner* world of the scientist's creative fantasy and the *outer* world of daily contingency.[41]

One can conclude that, where ancient civilizations studied the mystery of the cosmos in the sky as mirrored in the lakes, Banville studies the power of shape in the art of writing as mirrored in Kepler's theory. He produces an archaeological collage of scientific concepts in his work of art, in which the reader, observing the form, questions and problematizes the content. Banville goes beyond the limits of the non-representational and those imposed by postmodern aesthetics and subverts

---

[40] Arthur Koestler, *The Sleepwalkers*. p.419.
[41] Richard Kearney, *Transitions.Narratives in Modern Irish Culture*. P.94

them in his constant search for "new syntheses" that make more sense of the non-representational. The synthesis of mysticism and empiricism present in the scientist's work is transformed into an aesthetic synthesis, in which the intuitive shape of a work of art like *Kepler*, imposed from the outside and inviolable, becomes fused with the theme and other forms in the art of narrating:

> ...I have tried in my novels on Copernicus and Kepler not only to portray the men and their times, but more importantly, to illustrate something of their ideas by an orchestration of formal movement and rhythm in the prose. It is not for me to say how well, or how little, I have succeeded. Much more needs to be done. I think I can discern, very faintly, a new kind of novel, a new definition of fiction. Large efforts will be required, on the part of readers no less than writers.[42]

Banville shows how the fictional Copernicus and Kepler try to recuperate marginalized and repressed knowledge from the past, deconstructing possible "truths" in the same way as the historical scientists did. These universal and unquestionable "truths" which were also defended by Tycho Brahe, such as the principle of uniform velocity, the planets' perfect circular movement around the Sun, the denial of the existence of sunspots, were destroyed through intuitive revelations and *a priori* reasoning. Sometimes such revelations were supported by incorrect formulae but they nonetheless proved fertile as they pointed out other relative truths.

> Fiction is too imprecise a discipline to experience the kind of upheaval that relativity theory caused in physics, but all the same, something is happening, there are rumblings. The old certainties are going. In their place can come a new poetic intensity, once the form is freed of its obligations to psychologize, to spin yarns, to portray "reality." How the change will come about no one yet knows. But as science moves away from the search for blank certainties it takes on more and more the character of poetic metaphor, and since fiction is moving, however sluggishly, in the same direction, perhaps a certain seepage between the two streams is inevitable.[43]

---

[42] John Banville, "Physics and Fiction: Order from Chaos". In: *The New York Times Book Review*. April 21, 1985, p.42.
[43] John Banville, "Physics and Fiction: Order from Chaos". *The New York Times Book Review*, 1985. p.42.

Banville exalts shape, simultaneously deconstructing it internally. The *outer* fictional geometric structure remains only to be questioned and broken down in the third book of the tetralogy, *The Newton Letter*. The book was written in the epistolary form and subverted all the assumptions upon which the conception of a mechanicist and predictable world was based. Its aim is to expose the void present in the fictional truth of historical discourse.

The Revelation of Fictional Truth

At the beginning of each novel in the tetralogy, Banville introduces the paradigms upon which he will construct the pillars of his fiction. From this starting point the writer moves across the frontiers of various genres of fiction, biography, science and history and problematizes the validity of these narratives and their discourses. The first paragraph of *Doctor Copernicus* introduces the problematization of the words and the things in descriptive science, questioning their significance and showing the position of the character facing the enigma when he was a child. *Kepler* opens with various paradoxical elements in the scientist's dream which are then deconstructed throughout the whole book: the solution to the cosmic mystery is dreamed by Kepler, revealing the confrontation between intuition/revelation and science. This mystery is held in his mind as though it were a precious frail thing *"cupped in his hands"*, an image which Rüdiger Imhof[44] associates with the shape of the globe and the spheres of the individual planets, involving all the others that are nearer the Sun. Imhof also relates it to the finite cosmos and the fantastic construction of regular polygons within other polygons that exists in the globe constituted by fixed stars. Interpretations of the "constructed real" always create new epistemological

---

[44]Rüdiger Imhof, "John Banville's Supreme Fiction". In: IUR Vol11, No.1, 1981. pp.74-75.

metaphors, which are, in their term, re-interpreted by various discourses, in diverse contexts, constructing new significative syntheses.

In their search for truth, the fictional scientists foresee *a priori* solutions in a mythical way. Golden birds or angels reveal metaphorically the *jump* towards the infinite of Copernicus's creative act, or Kepler's *instinctus divinus*. Banville re-reads the scientists' beliefs and interprets the revelation of their "truths" aesthetically:

> He rose in the dawning grey gloom and lifted aside the drapes. Clouds were breaking to the east over a sullen waterscape. Calmly then it came, the solution, like a magnificent great slow golden bird alighting in his head with a thrumming of vast wings. It was so simple, so ravishingly simple, that at first he did not recognise it for what it was. (*D.C.* p.96)

Banville's Copernicus knows that he has to verify his theory after its revelation, and what matters will be the combination of the propositions, not the propositions themselves. This is indeed "the act of creation". The solution is *"the real thing"*, the live thing independent from the word.

In *Kepler*, the solution is always achieved *through the "back door of the mind"* as the historical scientist described in *Harmonice Mundi*. The solution came to him in a dream and he gained access to its laws through intuition, which he called *"that mythic bird"* or *"an announcing angel"* murmuring in his ear and revealing the existence of a God communicating with the chosen:

> And why had this annunciation been made to him, what heaven-hurled angel had whispered in his ear? He marvelled at the process, how a part of his mind had worked away in secret and in silence while the rest of him swilled and capered and lusted after poxed whores.(*K.*, p.73)

Copernicus and Kepler both believed in the final revelation, redemptive for the former and incarnated in his dead brother's ghost which calls to him on his deathbed, and illuminating for the latter:

> ... the angel of redemption an unlikely angel, I grant you, with dreadfully damaged wings, yet a redeemer" - (*C.*, p.249)

> Everything is told us, but nothing explained. Yes. We must take it all on trust. That's the secret. How simple! He smiled. It was not a mere book that was thus thrown away, but the foundation of a life's work. It seemed not to matter.(*K.* p. 185)

These revelations, which take place at the metaphysical moment of their passage from life to death, disclose the "truths" to which they had been dedicated throughout their lives, irrespective of personal discomfort. They are creative constructions of their minds, which Banville deconstructs and explores on a metafictional level because they are "supreme fictions".

In my opinion, the supreme revelation occurs in *The Newton Letter*, in the very process of deconstruction, when the synthesis of the scientist is applied to history, thus relating science to fiction. Imhof analyses the aesthetic value of this book, comparing it with canonical writings such as *The Sacred Fount* and *The Europeans* by Henry James, "Ein Brief" by Hofmannsthal, *Die Wahlverwandtschafen* (*Elective Affinities*) by Goethe, *The Good Soldier* by Ford Madox Ford, and *La Nausée* by Sartre; whereas McMinn believes that a synthesis is being postulated by Banville: *"a Big House version of the scientific mind"*.[45] On the other hand, my own analysis focuses on the way in which the experience of the theory of reversibility subverts its own principles and seeks to reveal how Banville creates a space within which he can question not only historical but also fictional (un)truth through a pseudo-epistolary narrative.

The letter Newton wrote to John Locke accusing him of conspiracy and treason, and of being involved with women, introduces the principle of the law of gravity in the construction of the "novella". It is also the centre of the centripetal and centrifugal forces that keep fiction and history in orbit. The anonymous narrator starts his letter confessing his failure to the Muse of History, *"Words fail me,*

---

[45] Joseph McMINN, *John Banville. A Critical Study.* p.90.

Clio" (...), and he affirms, *"Shall I say, I've lost my faith in the primacy of text?".*[46] The historian is in conflict both with himself and with the art of narrating the truths of the past or, more precisely, with the science of "making history", when he discovers the impossibility of deducing the causes of human behavioural phenomena. This crisis occurs when he attempts to apply universal laws governing the exterior world to the interior world:

> But Clio, dear Cliona, you have been my teacher and my friend, my inspiration, for too long, I couldn't lie to you. Which doesn't mean I know what the truth is, and how to tell it to you. (*T.N.L.*, p.10)

This quotation is directly related to Banville's belief in the interaction between the liar and the listener which is provoked by the shared lie which is sublimated as a ritual and, paradoxically, constructs supreme fictions.[47]

The third book of the tetralogy, *The Newton Letter,* is a satire within three tragedies, as Banville said when he compared it to the Greek form. It subverts the absolute and predictable Newtonian truths to make way for fictional truths within the historical narratives themselves. This novel has the same function as the musical form that is referred to in the subtitle, "An Interlude". It is an *"intermezzo"* that is inserted in between the various parts of a long composition. Banville declares, *"My readers, that small band, deserve a rest."* [48]

The narrator, a historian, is trying to conclude the biography of Isaac Newton, looking for the causes of the scientist's nervous collapse in the letters he wrote to John Locke (one real and the other fictitious, based on *Ein Brief* by Hugo Von Hofmannsthal - "The Letter of Lord Chandos"[49]). When he has to cross the frontiers of reality in order to explain the historical fact through the analyses of the documents in hand, he discovers the invalidity of reaching a "historical truth". To prove this, he focuses his narrative upon the experiences of his own personal

---

[46] John Banville, *The Newton Letter*. p.9.
[47] See John Banville. "A Talk". In: *IUR*, Vol.11, No.1, 1981. p.16.
[48] Rüdiger Imhof, "An Interview with John Banville". In: *IUR*. Vol. 11, N° 1, 1981. p12.
[49] Banville mentions the source at the end of the *"novella"*.

history in an analogical way. According to McMinn, he does not believe in the value of interpretation any more, and he re-enacts the history of his own book, in which two simultaneous stories are narrated: one being the biographical recreation of Newton's crisis, and the other occurring in contemporary Ireland.

Banville plays with the absolute truths of space, time and motion upon which Newton constructed his concept of the universe. The fictional narrative, which is concerned with the question of the validity of the description of facts and the objective interpretation of history, subverts the mechanistic vision of the world and deconstructs the idea of Nature as automaton with phenomena occurring in a linear sequence according to a cause-effect determinism. *The Newton Letter* is, therefore, a satire on the Positivism that places historians beside scientists as guardians of an objective truth. The scientific limits of historical truth are transposed to a fictional space, as was the case with scientific truth in the first two books of the tetralogy. However, this fictional "truth" is also questioned, in the form of a satire which will be understood by those readers with "cute ears" while others will only laugh:

> I am confused. I feel ridiculous and melodramatic, and comically exposed. I have shinned up to this high perch and can't see how to get down, and of the spectators below, some are embarrassed and the rest are about to start laughing. (*T.N.L.*, p.10)

Banville reverses the Newtonian synthesis which shows an alliance between the rational comprehension of nature and its practical manipulation. To do this, he adopts the scientist's technique of isolating a specific phenomenon and uses it as the basis for the deduction of other groups of phenomena occurring in similar circumstances. Thus, the fictionist re-uses elements that appeared in *Birchwood*, such as the Big House, the assumptions of that age and the name of the family (the Lawlesses), and he manipulates them to prove the scientific theory of prediction.

The narrator rents a roadside lodge, part of a Big House – Fern House, near Dublin. He wants to isolate himself there in order to finish writing the biography of Sir Isaac Newton, but he abandons it after a few weeks, just as the scientist had done with his research:

> There was no fiery revelation to account for my crisis of faith; there was not even what could properly be called a crisis. Only, I wasn't working now. (...) You won't believe me, I know: how could I drop seven years of work, just like that? Newton was my life, not these dull pale people in their tumbledown house in the hollow heart of the country. But I didn't see it as this stark alternative: things take a definite and simple shape only in retrospect.(*T.N.L.*, pp. 31-32)

Edward and Charlotte live in the main house with their niece, Ottilie, and Michael, their adopted child. As he has always been attracted by the "insistent enigma of other people", the narrator makes an interpretative reading of the people following the law of reversibility: a typical Protestant family in a pastoral context, living in a Big House in decay.

According to Newton's mechanicist conception of the world, time is reversible and the law of reversibility determines the future just as it determined the past. In *Order Out of Chaos*, Prigogine and Stengers conclude that Newton synthesises "being and becoming". The metaphor that represents this theory is the clock, and its major implication is the inference that the world as a machine has a fixed and static form and, once it has been set in motion, it will continue for ever without the need of divine intervention. This image appears in the fictional narrative many times - *"through opposing doors, Charlotte and Ottilie swept in, like mechanical figures in a clock tower"* (81).

This causal process that permits phenomena to be related to an organizing principle, determines its future coherence and unity. The astonished narrator expresses wonderment in the face of "visions":

> I, whose passion is the past, was discovering in her [Ottilie] what the past means. And not just the past. Before our affair - the word makes me wince - before it had properly begun I was contemplating the end of it. You'll laugh, but I used to picture my deathbed... (*T.N.L.*, p.38)

The predictable future establishes a symbolic relationship between simultaneous or successive phenomena. Banville closes his fictional interlude with an interrogative discourse as a way of simultaneously affirming and subverting scientific theory. The narrator flees his exile in the countryside because he is unable to experience the equilibrium of the natural forces of the human being repeating themselves in space *in eternum*. Nevertheless, he realizes that he will return to the same place though this time to question the dilemma of the truth of mechanistic Nature:

> Go back to Ferns, move in, set up house, fulfil some grand design, with Ottilie, poor Charlotte, the two boys - for I feel it will be a boy, it must be - become a nurseryman and wear tweeds, talk about the weather, stand around chewing a straw? Impossible. All the same, I shall go back. And in the end, it's come to me just this moment, in the end of course I shall take up the book and finish it: such a renunciation is not of this world. Yet I'm wary. Shall I have to go off again, leaving my research, my book and everything else unfinished? Shall I awake in a few months, in a few years, broken and deceived, in the midst of new ruins?

This passage suggests a Foucauldian inference in relation to predictable facts that shows the sovereignty of a collective conscience as the principle of unity and of explication, the "common sense" that separates the subject from the object, that moves in space and time in a linear way. This common sense is essential in the application of inductive-deductive reasoning to the interpretation of facts and the unveiling of the mystery of commonality, not of the exotic. Ever since he was a child, the narrator has felt the law of attraction by the enigma of the Other:

> I would gaze at that silent house and wonder, in a hunger of curiosity, what lives were lived there. Who stacked that firewood, hung that holly wreath, left those tracks in the hoarfrost on the hill? I can't express the odd aching pleasure of that moment. I knew, of course, that those hidden lives wouldn't be much different from my own. But that was the point. It wasn't the exotic I was after, but the ordinary, that strangest and most elusive of enigmas. (*T.N.L.*, p.19)

However, in the personal story of the narrator, the "absolute truths" apprehended by common sense dissipate, and the idea of a predictable nature under human control is checkmated at every destroyed assumption. Edward is neither a *bon vivant* nor an opportunist who married the daughter of the owner of Fern House, but he is dying of cancer; Charlotte is apparently terribly refined and distant, as those in high society generally are, but this is the result of high doses of Valium prescribed by her doctor, Ottilie is the daughter of Charlotte's brother who had died with his wife in a car accident, and Michael is child adopted by the couple, which means that he is neither their son nor the bastard son of Edward and Ottilie, as he himself imagines:

> I was like an embarrassed anthropologist realising that what he had for months taken to be the ordinary muddle of tribal life is really an immense intricate ceremony, in which the tiniest gesture is foreordained and vital, in which he is the only part that does not fit. (*T.N.L.* p.68)

The anonymous historian abandons his intention of finishing his book because he perceives that, in his own personal story, the current facts reveal lying truths. The oxymoron "fictitious truths", used by Riffaterre in *Fictional Truth*,[50] helps us to understand the paradox. The narrator wonders about the "true constructions" of the present. If they are inferred erroneously in the process of interpretation, according to the universal law, the abyss between truth and its construction (the "untruth") will be greater when facts from the past are analysed. The narrator-historian fails in his attempt to reconstruct what had happened to Edward in the time between the closing of the town pubs and his return to home. Because of this he abandons his work - "*. . . what occurred in those 'lost' hours, we can only speculate. (...) I can't go on. I'm not a historian anymore"* (80).

It is at this crossroad that Banville places his interlude, *The Newton Letter,* to question the "objectivity" of a purely descriptive "historizing history", and of the dynamic historicism which, according to Adam Schaff in *História e Verdade*,

---
[50]Michael Riffaterre, *Fictional Truth.* p.1-4.

implies capturing nature, society and human beings in motion. Historicism leads to the denial of the absolute principles because the historian must relate ideas to historical conditions. The caricaturesque description of the historian Popov, which contains some quotations from Newton's biography, clearly shows the contrast of the two forms of producing history:

> I met him once, an awful little man with ferret eyes and a greasy suit. Reminded me of an embalmer. Which, come to think of it, is apt. I like his disclaimer: *Before the phenomenon of Isaac Newton, the historian, like Freud when he came to contemplate Leonardo, can only shake his head and retire with as much good grace as he can muster.* Then out come the syringe and the formalin. That is what I was doing too, embalming old N.'s big corpse, only I *did* have the grace to pop off before the deathshead grin was properly fixed.
> *Newton was the greatest genius that science has produced.* Well, who would deny it? (*T.N.L.*, p.29)

The fictional historian rebels against the descriptive function of the facts, which reveals the stagnation and dissection of science when seen from this perspective. This is due to the absence of theory that precedes the act of writing history, which gives it sense, an object, a cause, and an aim. He explains his own theory at the beginning of the novel when he justifies the aim of his book:

> Oh yes, you can see, can't you, the outline of what my book would have been, a celebration of action, of the scientist as hero, a gleeful acceptance of Pandora's fearful disclosures, wishy-washy medievalism kicked out and the age of reason restored. But would you believe that all this, this Popovian Newton-as-the-greatest-scientist-the-world-has-known, now makes me feel slightly sick? Not that I think any of it untrue, in the sense that it is fact. It's just that another kind of truth has come to seem to me more urgent, although, for the mind, it is nothing compared to the lofty verities of science. (*T.N.L.*, pp.29-30)

History means interpretation. E. H. Carr says that the reader should listen to the historian's voice with care, because "history is interpretation".[51] Lucien Febvre adds that, in fact, history is a choice, not an arbitrary but a pre-conceived one.

---

[51] In: Adam Schaff, *História e Verdade*. pp.235-6.

According to him, without a pre-conceived theory there is no scientific work. A historian cannot submit to the facts as though they had not been constructed and selected by himself.

In his masterpiece, *Principia,* the historical Newton shows the contrast that can exist between the objective importance of a discovery and the subjective meaning given to it by its author.[52] It is for this reason that Schaff argues that historical facts are manifestations selected from many others due to the relationship between cause and effect and to their position on the map of greater totalities. The criterion of choice gives meaning to the fact and presupposes a system of reference where evaluation and selection take place and endow the historical fact with relativism.

The letter to Clio, in which he tries to understand why he has abandoned the book, is an explanatory repetition of the historian's hypothesis concerning the cause of Newton's nervous collapse in the summer of 1693 and why he devoted himself to the interpretative study of the Bible and alchemy, a fact that never fails to embarrass his historians. He focuses upon the analysis of the two letters that Newton wrote to Locke (the second is fictitious), comparing the closures and signatures with *"morbid fascination"*:

> *I am your most humble and unfortunate servant, Is. Newton.*(*T.N.L.*, p.13)

> Then comes that cold, that brave, that almost carven signature: *Newton.* *(T.B.E.,* p.59*)*

In historiographic analysis, the subjective factor lies in the selection of the fact and the theory that precedes the interpretative process. The choice and the logic enchaining facts to "explain" history are controlled by the spirit that selects and gathers them:

> It seems to me to express better than anything that has gone before it Newton's pain and anguished bafflement. I compare it to the way a few weeks later he signed, with just the stark surname, another, and altogether

---

[52]Hans Reichenbach, *From Copernicus to Einstein.*

different, letter. What happened in the interval, what knowledge dawned on him?
We have speculated a great deal, you and I, on his nervous collapse late in that summer of '93. (*T.N.L.*, p.13)

The historian adopts the method of historical materialism that approaches the object of study as a monad, although he believes that history is the "celebration of action". As Walter Benjamin says, thinking does not only include the movement of ideas but also their immobilisation.[53] The narrator concentrates his thought on a configuration saturated with tensions, the letter to Locke, which crystalizes in a monad in order to be able to recapture a past that has been silenced and to hear the echo of a voice that has become mute due to the fluctuating political powers of history. In "In the beginning were the words", Banville quotes a passage from Hugo von Hofmannsthal's "Letter of Lord Chandos":

> I feel...that the language in which it may be given me not only to write, but also to think, will be not Latin, or English, or Italian, or Spanish, but a language not one of whose words I know, a language in which mute things speak to me, and in which, it may be, I shall at last have to defend myself after death before an unknown judge.[54]

The second letter to Locke, the fictitious one, is based on the letter of Lord Chandos and reproduces the words above which, according to the narrator, reveal Newton's attempt to understand and express his inner self. He considers it to be the centre not only of his own work but also of the scientist's, *"reflecting and containing all the rest, as the image of Charlotte contained, as in a convex mirror, the entire world of Ferns"* (58-59). In this way, the letter, which is repeated many times since it is also at the centre of Banville's work, is deconstructed in relation to a historical and fictional truth which questions the meanings generated by the relationship between facts and the language that expresses them. As in *Doctor*

---

[53] Walter Benjamin, *Magia e Técnica*. Arte e Política. p.231.
[54] In: *Weekend Guardian*. July 7-8, 1990. p.20.

Copernicus and *Kepler*, the narrator echoes the end of the fictitious letter looking for its "true" meaning:

> *My dear Doctor, expect no more philosophy from my pen. The language in which I might be able not only to write but to think is neither Latin nor English, but a language none of whose words is known to me; a language in which common place things speak to me; and wherein I may one day have to justify myself before an unknown judge.* Then comes that cold, that brave, that almost carven signature: *Newton*. What did he mean, what was it those commonplace things said to him, what secret did they impart? And so I sat in the shadow of lilacs, nursing an unrequitable love and reading a dead man's testament, trying to understand it. (*N.L.*, pp. 60-61)

This passage shows the reproduction of the fictitious to be a form of fictional truth, also destabilizing the historical truth. Where the specificity of the historical narrative shows the accumulation of relative truths that lead to the absolute truth, the historical one becomes fictional, constructed according to systems of reference and evaluative criteria chosen by the writer himself.

In *Fictional Truth*, Riffaterre affirms that fictional truth belongs to the field of fiction as a genre, and contrary to what was believed traditionally, it does not depend on verisimilitude. *The Newton Letter* thus subverts that verisimilitude or *mimesis* of reality, introducing another fictional truth which is conceived as a linguistic phenomenon directly dependent upon the text.

In the historical narrative, different visions and various discourses, sometimes contradictory, construct relative truths that are interpreted according to their context. According to Riffaterre, the discourse of fictional truth is external and parallel to the narrative; it is a metalanguage and depends directly on the logical imperatives of assumptions and conclusions.[55] Just as Newton succeeds in making a synthesis of Kepler's and Galileo's principles and in discovering *a posteriori* the universal law of gravity, as well as improving the concepts of optics, so Banville makes a synthesis of the eighteenth-century and postmodern thought. He deconstructs the knowledge that was based on fossilised principles rooted in the

---
[55] Michael Riffaterre, *Fictional Truth*. pp. 84--85.

notion of linearity, and he subverts them in relation to their origin, using the same principles of Newtonian synthesis now applied to the art of writing fiction.

Banville passes from the former mechanistic vision of the universe to the romantic image of the world as an organism that transforms itself through the vivid force of the nineteenth century. But in his next novel, *Mefisto*, he portrays the effects of Einstein's theory of relativity[56] in counterpoint to the theory of evolution. The latter represents the dynamic concept of changes where the whole is not the sum of the parts but a *vivid force*. For Einstein, time is relative not because the universe is alive but because the motion of the observer affects the descriptive language. In the field of quantum theory, Fritjof Capra, the prophet of the holistic vision of the world, shows the world to be a dynamic web of inseparable energy structures. There is only a one-way interaction in the relation of cause-effect; nevertheless, when every cause is simultaneously an effect and each effect is, in its turn, a cause, the interaction is multidirectional. *Mefisto* is the reflection of the synthesis of chaos and order that exists in the real world just as it does in the field of fiction.

Order Out of Chaos

I mentioned previously that, according to Banville, the aim of a work of art is not to "save" the phenomenon but to lose or to risk losing it. I hope my analysis of The Newton Letter has made it clear that Banville subverts the fictional truth that tries to "save" fiction as a representation of reality, to "save" verisimilitude to the detriment of a "supra-reality" which shows an intensity of action that does not exist in a real context.

---

[56] In "Physics and Fiction: Order from Chaos", Banville says: *"...imagine a Nabokov novel based on the life of a Gödel or an Einstein!"*. In: *The New York Book Review*, 1985.

M.C. Escher, "Order and Chaos"

(lithograph, 1950)

In: Hofstadter, D. *Gödel, Escher, Bach: An Eternal Golden Braid.*
New York: Vintage Books, 1980.

In the tetralogy, Banville shows how the scientists failed to perceive the simplest facts in trying to "save" and explain the phenomena. Andrea's disembodied voice says to the agonising Copernicus, *"But you tried to discard the commonplace truths for the transcendent ideas, and so failed."* On his death-bed Kepler recognises the meaning of the Jew's words, *"Everything is told us, but nothing is explained. Yes. We must take it all on trust. That's the secret. How simple!"* The narrator of *The Newton Letter* writes, *"I dreamed up a horrid drama, and failed to see the commonplace tragedy that was playing itself out in real life".*

The tetralogy was written as an attempt to recreate aesthetically the universal force in human history that moves humans in their search for order, for a synthesis of a reality that can neither be controlled nor grasped because "truth" is immersed in chaos. The fictitious Copernicus marvels at the mysterious desire of the gnostic Trismegistus to find a redemptive universal unity in the chaos of the world. Through Rheticus's voice he says that, when an observer has already had a vision of chaos, something is placed in between:

> . . . and so you make a mirror, thinking that in it shall be reflected the reality of the world; but then you understand that the mirror reflects only appearances, and that reality is somewhere else, off behind the mirror; and then you remember that behind the mirror there is only the chaos. (*C.*, p.222)

Banville argues that contemporary science depicts a chaotic world although, inside every human being, there is *"a separate reality, which has shape and significance, which we think of as some sort of truth, and which is endowed with a beginning, middle and an end."*[57] He adds that it is our desire to see this inward reality made manifest in the external world. This is what Wallace Stevens described as our *"rage for order"*. Banville's idea echoes the historical Kepler, who believed in a universal order and harmony, which materialises in the voice of

---

[57] John Banville, "Physics and Fiction: Order from Chaos". In: The New York Times Book Review, April 1985. p.41.

the fictitious Kepler when he writes to his daughter Regina about the meaning of life. Life is shapeless and each person has to mould it into a *"perfect sphere"* that contains himself. He continues,

> That, so I thought, is our task here, I mean the transformation of the chaos without, into a perfect harmony & balance within us. Wrong, wrong: for our lives contain us, we are the flaw in the crystal, the speck of grit which must be ejected from the spinning sphere".(*K.*, p.131).

Newtonian science presents a mechanicist, determinist and objective vision of nature as it contains no reference to the observer and leaves no space for the unpredictable, thus becoming an atemporal science. But, static time produces a conflict with existential time, between being and becoming. The narrator/historiographer in *The Newton Letter* suffers a dislocation when he analyses the fusion of two persons into one, "Charlottilie", when he makes love with Ottilie imagining that she is Charlotte. This sense of dislocation results in a notion of time and space which he finds difficult to explain:

> It was the notion of a time out of time, of this summer as a self-contained unit separate from the time of the ordinary world. (...) The future had ceased to exist. I drifted, lolling like a Dead Sea swimmer, lapped round by a warm blue soup of timelessness. (*T.N.L.*, p.58)

He perceives that his mechanical interpretation of human behaviour fails when the law of reversibility is applied to facts. If there is no certainty about some facts and if they sometimes cause irreversible processes, does this mean that it is possible for irreversible facts to increase in the process of historical interpretation when unpredictability occurs?

The implications of an increase of entropy, which is the basis of the Second Law of Thermodynamics, the complex nineteenth-century science that studies the transformation of motion into heat and vice versa, explain the existence of the reversible and irreversible systems that help the reader to understand Banville's questions as raised by the narrator in *The Newton Letter*. If the First Law of

Thermodynamics proved the conservation of energy, the Second Law introduced the idea of irreversible processes, of an "arrow of time" because there is a diffusion of heat that cannot be recovered in mechanical energy. This revelation also occurs in the field of fictional truth when the fictional historian recognises that he has based his interpretation on the observation of each member of the family as though they are separate entities, when in reality they are part of a common organism:

> I hadn't thought of them as husband and wife, mother, son, niece, aunt - aunt! - but now suddenly they were a family, a closed, mysterious organism. Amazing questions occurred to me. What really did they mean to each other?. (*T.N.L.*, p.67)

This questioning of what the family members mean to each other shows, by analogy, the road to interrogative nineteenth-century Physics when it established a new dialogue with nature. It was perceived that reversible processes interact with the irreversible ones that had been considered exceptions by classical science. The interchange between machine and environment produced the concept of entropy – the natural degree of disorder which reveals the evolution of time, "the arrow of time". Entropy is the recurrence of irreversible changes within a system. But, instead of generating disorder (the mechanical interpretation of the Second Law of Thermodynamics in the nineteenth century was represented by a worn machine), there is a recent theory that reveals irreversible processes to be a source of order: *"order out of chaos."* In the second half of our century, Prigogine and Stengers proposed a new synthesis that subverted the previous interpretation, encompassing reversible and irreversible time, order and disorder, Physics and Biology, chance and necessity. Current thought about the conception of the universe thus argues that entropy produces the paradox that chaos is also a process of order, organisation and life.

In the last book of his tetralogy, Banville immerses himself in these paradoxes, taking as his parameter the doubts that generated the scientific changes that occurred at the beginning of the twentieth century. When Banville was asked about his new book he answered that it was about a modern physicist, *"someone somewhere between Einstein and Eisenberg."*[58] Imhof argues that Einstein is Banville's model quoting from "Physics and Fiction: Order from Chaos" where Banville invites the reader to imagine a *"Nabokov novel based on the life of a Gödel or an Einstein!"* [59]:

> In point of fact, precocious Swan does not truly resemble Einstein, who when young showed no visible signs of any special precocity and never developed any interest in mathematical puzzles. Yet he is like Einstein inasmuch as his feelings about the mysterious order that seems to underly the apparent chaos of events - the discovery that nature appears to present itself as a mathematical riddle with remarkably simple and elegant solutions - were formed in his childhood.[60]

Einstein developed two revolutionary concepts, the theory of relativity and the interpretation of electromagnetic radiation, which gave rise to quantum theory. In *The Turning Point*, Fritjof Capra says that Einstein believed in the inherent harmony of nature and sought to perfect a unified field theory that would represent a four-dimensional structure for the universe where gravitation and electromagnetism were aspects of space-time geometry. At the beginning of the century, scientists were struggling to apprehend nature in a way that would resolve the paradoxes they perceived. They were aware that their basic concepts, language and way of thinking were inadequate to describe atomic phenomena.[61] Thus, scientists went through the same labyrinths and faced the same crossroads as their ancestors, as Banville shows in *Doctor Copernicus* and *Kepler*.

The Newton Letter represents the transition of human thought from the mechanicist Cartesian world-view originated by Newton, to a *holistic* view of a dynamic, indivisible whole whose parts are interrelated and can only be analysed within a cosmic process.

---

[58] "Nothing to Say!".
[59] In: *The New York Times Book Review*, April 21, 1985. p.42
[60] Rüdiger Imhoff, p.153.

Mefisto, the last novel in the tetralogy, represents the dark side of the human mind – the anxiety of uncertainty generated by the unpredictable, the void of loss in irreversible processes, where death is the result of maximum entropy. Scientifically, the law of probability present in irreversible processes leads to the concept of chance and to the coexistence of chance and necessity. It is at this "turning point", where chance is considered to be a constituent of nature, that Banville begins the concluding volume of his tetralogy, using the voice of the narrator as a mediator for his subversions: *"Chance was in the beginning."*

Banville places chance at the beginning and end of his circular narrative and deconstructs its significance on various levels. In *Lógica do Pior*, Clément Rosset defines the tragic and silent concept of chance based on Bergson's theory. Bergson describes chaos as chance, arguing that chaos is not a disordered world but an *"x"* before any idea of order or disorder.[62] He sees chance as existing prior to any necessity or variation of order. According to Rosset, it is important to distinguish between four different levels in the genesis of the idea of chance, which range from less causal to more causal effects, if 'chance' defines not a silent concept but a concept that tends endlessly towards silence.[63]

In this way, Banville portrays the notions of luck, encounter, contingency and pure chance to signify the act of denial, without referring exactly to what it is denied. He uses fictional narrative to interact with the doctrine of relativity, of simultaneity, reviewing his previous novels, especially *Birchwood*, in order to mold a new fictional synthesis, to create a significance, a Prigoginian order whose starting point is chaos:

> Order, pattern, harmony. Press hard enough upon anything, upon everything, and the random would be resolved. I waited, impatient, in a state of grim elation. I had thrown out the accumulated impedimenta of years, I was after simplicity now, the pure, uncluttered thing. Everywhere were secret signs. The machine sang to me, for was not I too built on a binary code? One and zero, these were the poles. (*M.* p.202)

---

[61] Fritjof Capra, pp.70-71
[62] Clément Rosset, C. *Lógica do Pior.* p.83.
[63] *Ibid.*, p.84

Banville divides his book into two parts; in the first one, entitled "Marionettes", Gabriel Swan, the narrator, who was born with the gift of numbers, recounts his childhood and adolescence, portraying people as if they were marionettes in the hands of chance. He narrates how he meets the new dwellers of Ashborn (a "Big House" just like in *Birchwood*) where his mother had been born when his father Jack Kay was working there. He describes his relationships with Sophie, a deaf and dumb girl, with Felix (Mefisto), who exerts a strong control over the others, and with Mr. Kasperl, who manages the mine workers and spends hours calculating in a black notebook. In the second part, entitled "Angels", Gabriel narrates his sufferings after being re-born from the ashes as a phoenix. He had nearly been burnt alive when Ashburn was destroyed and sublimated by a fire. He also describes his life in hospital, how he becomes a drug-addict due to the unbearable pain, and his re-encounter with Felix in town who introduces him to Professor Kosok who is working on a computer-project *"searching for the meaning of life"*. The narrator thus focuses on the sub-world of drugs that Gabriel shares with Adele, the professor's daughter, Felix and his friends.

In their analysis of *Mefisto*, Imhoff and McMinn compare the novel with Goethe's *Faustus* and explore the self-referentiality of *Birchwood*. Although these are interesting themes, I believe that the originality of this last book in the tetralogy lies in the portrait that Banville paints of the agony of the human mind when it faces chaos, a vision that he anticipated in *Copernicus*. The tragic experience of chance leads to a synthesis whose main constituents are fiction, science and philosophy. According to Banville, art is the search for an implicit order in chaos. Through art, the writer exerts the power of selection at various points of bifurcation that occur along the "arrow of time". Thus, he plays with possible future states in a microcosmos which also reveals the interaction between necessity and chance in the art of writing.

Banville opens the novel with the first concept of chance: the concept of luck that is applied to an *"x"* called fortune, the origin of a causal series which could be either happy or unhappy. The mythopoetic description of the narrator shows him as a "tiny swimmer" coming out of a catastrophe when Castor, the Polydeuces, lies dead in the white room. This reference to the twin gods of earth and heaven, Castor and Pollux, sons of Leda and Zeus (the swan), produces many resonances as the narrative evolves because, when Castor dies, Pollux can find no consolation and decides to share his immortality with his brother. Chance, in the form of luck, is a constituent of nature. It grants life to one of the twins and denies it to the other. It is the beginning and the end, *"the end also was chance"*. The narrator hesitates between the two opposite poles: the fortune of being alive (the fortuitous chance, the absolutely non-necessary according to Rosset) and its contrary, destiny, the absolutely necessary – the death of the twin brother:

> I don't know when it was that I first heard of the existence, if that's the word, of my dead brother. From the start I knew I was the survivor of some small catastrophe, the shock-waves were still reverberating faintly inside me.(*M.*, p.8)

Luck also appears in the second part of the book, "Angels", but this time in the form of a series of unhappy causes that give rise to the tragic chance. Felix invites Gabriel to a party when the latter has just left hospital with a supply of the "Lamias" drug. Felix shouts ironically "What a lucky chance". The chain of events in the second part shows Felix's aim in taking Gabriel to a bar where drugs circulate and are negotiated without any restriction. Professor Kosok also speaks about luck in his search for the meaning of life and, ironically, denies the existence of the patterns of order found by Gabriel. Leitch, the assistant, says to him, *"You're supposed to be the genius, you tell me. Statistics, probabilities, blind chance, I don't know. Why don't you ask him? He's half cracked, anyway"* (170). Felix had already alerted Gabriel that the blind luck the professor believed in did not really exist, *"Blind chance, he says, blind chance, that's all. As if chance was blind. We know better, don't we Castor?"* (162).

The concept of chance as encounter, as a point of intersection between two or more causal series, is explored through the theme of the divided self, revisited by

Banville in various novels, particularly in the image of the living twin in *Birchwood* and the dead one in *Mefisto*. Banville confesses that, for him, the way a twin can escape into another name and self while at the same time asserting a separate identity *"is a powerful metaphor for the act of fiction: in telling the story the writer too becomes someone else"*.[64] When two independent series meet unpredictably at a certain point in time and space, the referentials of that encounter are also unpredictable. This concept of simultaneity at a single point is linked to Einstein's theory of relativity. In *From Copernicus to Einstein*, Hans Reichenbach distinguishes simultaneity at a single point *"as a coincidence, as a 'point-event'"*, from simultaneous distant facts *"as a phenomenon spatially and temporally dimensionless"*.[65]

But, if we cannot prevent possible encounters between all existing series, the notion of chance, in the sense of making coincidences, of simultaneity, takes shape and serves to explain the idea of duality which precedes the notion of chance which already exists before any given encounter:

> When did my mother realise the nature of the cargo she was carrying? What archangel spoke? Dualities perhaps would fascinate her, glimpsed reflections, coincidences of course. A pair of magpies swaggering among the cabbages gave her a fright. Old sayings might strike her with a new significance: peas in a pod, two new pins, chalk and cheese. Maybe now and then she fancied she could hear us, horribly together in our crowded amniotic sea, crooning and tinily crying. (*M.*, p.4)

Duality is what the writer experiences during the process of creation. The simultaneity of feeling oneself to be two persons in one is expressed by Banville on the metafictional level. Gabriel denounces the presence of another in his self on various occasions, particularly when he analyses unpredictable personal reactions. For example, at Felix's request, Gabriel and Sophie perform a wedding pantomime; he wears the bride's dress and Sophie is the groom:

---

[64] Ciaran Carty, "Out of Chaos Comes order". In: *The Sunday Tribune*, 14 Sep. 1986. p.19.
[65] Hans Reichenbach, pp.57-58.

> It was as if inside this gown there was not myself but someone else, some other flesh, pliable, yielding, utterly at my mercy. Each trembling step I took was like the fitful writhing of a captive whom I held pressed tightly to my pitiless heart. I caught my reflection in a cracked bit of mirror on the wall, and for a second someone else looked at me, dazed and crazily grinning, from behind my own face. (*M.*, p.83)

The presence of the other lost "self" is perceived at the moments of greater tension that precede acts of chance, as occurs when he finds Adele unconscious under the effects of an overdose and he calls an ambulance to take her to hospital:

> I felt as if I were a stranger, I mean, a stranger to myself, as if there were two of us, I and that other, that interpoler standing up inside me, sharing in secret this pillar of frail flesh and pain. But then, I was not alone.
> She was in the dingy bathroom on the landing, . . . (*M.* p.197)

The notion of chance as *contingency* is also derived from the idea of simultaneity, not in the sense of *coincidence* but of *non-necessity*. This idea goes back to Einstein's theory of the simultaneity of distant events. Reichenbach argues that the scientist found a logical solution to the problem of judging simultaneity because, according to him, it can never be verified, only defined. It is arbitrary and the process can never lead to a contradiction.[66]

The principle of unpredictability governs contingency and the narrator emphasizes this kind of simultaneity, invalidating the processes of verification:

> It was here, in the big world, that I would meet what I was waiting for, that perfectly simple, ravishing, unchallengeable formula in the light of which the mask of mere contingency would melt." (*M.*, p.186)

The narrative of "Marionettes" is based on a series of causal events that coincide fortuitously or unpredictably. They either coincide or are absolutely non-necessary. They show the evolution of the narrator's mind which, although it is mathematical in nature, cannot verify the existence of the order, harmony, symmetry and completeness that he experiences in the presence of numbers. He

---

[66] Hans Reichenbach, From *Copernicus to Einstein*. p.60.

fails when he seeks to equate these qualities with distant phenomena. The reader observes a series of events (the encounter with the new owners of Ashburn, Gabriel's relationship with Sophie, whose first kiss awakens him to a risky and strange disordered world, the explosion of the mine, the car accident that killed his mother, the finding of the marionettes when the house was burning) which reveal the turning points caused by the constituent chance. The element of chance presupposes the existence of a nature consisting of causal exceptions which lead the narrator to lose his credibility in order to create space for the idea of chaos:

> Oh, I worked. Ashburn, Jack Kay, my mother, the black dog, the crash, all this, it was not like numbers, yet it too must have rules, order, some sort of pattern. Always I had thought of number falling on the chaos of things like frost falling on water, the seething particles tamed and sorted, the crystals locking, the frozen lattice spreading outwards in all directions. I could feel in my mind, the crunch of things coming to a stop, the creaking stillness, the stunned, white air. But marshal the factors how I might, they would not equate now. Everything was sway and flow and sudden lurch. Surfaces that had seemed solid began to give way under me. I could hold nothing in my hands, all slipped through my fingers helplessly. Zero, minus quantities, irrational numbers, the infinite itself, suddenly these things revealed themselves for what they really had been, always. I grew dizzy. The light retreated. A blackbird whistled in the glimmering dusk. I held my face in my hands, that too flowed away, the features melting, even the eyeholes filling up, until all that was left was a smooth blank mask of flesh. (*M.*, pp.109-110)

This long quotation reveals the causal series whose constituents fit together in (dis)order as though in a jig-saw puzzle, and contains the exact moment of transition from certainty to uncertainty, from order to the discovery of entropy which would produce mutations in a larger system. The sense of harmony and symmetry had been present in Gabriel's mind up until that moment, even when observing other people's work. When Gabriel reads Dr. Kasperl's black notebook, he marvels at his calculations, diagrams and algebraic formulae, even though they are incomprehensible to him. However, he misinterprets the features they have in common, a *"particular fondness for symmetries, for example, for mirror equivalences, and palindromic series"* (69). The revelation of the opposite is fictionalized with elements used by Banville in previous novels – darkness and the bird of revelation. But a blank mask of flesh and bones is the ghostly image provoked by emptiness and chaos. While Ashburn is burning, Gabriel discovers this mask while looking at the marionettes that represent the story of his life, particularly the one personifying himself. Blankness appears in the midst of this tragedy and establishes closer ties to the *original* chance.

Tragic thought, a constituent of chance, is incompatible with any kind of intervention and discloses a loss of reference that comes an instant before its construction, as Rosset has defined it.[67] "Angels" is a narrative that moves from the *constituted* chance (where there is a primary nature that brings it into existence, either luck or contingency) to *constituent* chance (which is the original producer of all forms of existence). It is necessary to understand the materialist-philosophical concept of chance in order to be able to apply it to the complete analysis of *Mefisto*. This concept refers to the capacity of matter to organise itself spontaneously as inert matter receives life, movement and different forms of order by chance.[68] This idea is anathema to those who hold the materialistic concept of chance, as it negates the notion of being and familiarisation since the known, the familiar, becomes unexpectedly unknown.

Gabriel immerses himself in the data received by the computer in a search for intricate patterns of correspondence and repetition, but Professor Kosok does not accept these patterns because of the horrific estrangement that the self-generation of order out chaos would provoke:

> But he seemed to want only disconnected bits, oases of order in a desert of randomness. When I attempted to map out a general pattern he grew surly, and threw down his pencil on the console and stamped away, fuming. (*M.*, p.170)

---

[67] Clément Rosset, *Lógica do pior*. p.89.
[68] *Ibid.*, p.97.

For Gabriel everything is part of a pattern, *"From the start the world had been for me an immense formula"*. Nevertheless, during his recovery in hospital, his disequilibrium, caused by pain and the unpredictable, makes him panic at the idea of falling into the abyss of thought, of disconnected numbers, of chaos:

> Now I could not sleep, I who had slept for so long. I built up walls of number, brick on brick, to keep the pain out. They all fell down. Equations broke in half, zeros gaped like holes. Always I was left amid rubble, facing into the dark. (*M.* p.127)

Pain becomes part of his self, and it is this duality that is always present, preceding chance itself. It is *"a sort of second, ghostly self"*. Pain has a smell, a sound of suffering and, at the same time, a deep, communing silence. The discovery of death as the original chance gives birth to the idea of absolute absence:

> That was death. No cowled dark stranger, no kindly friend, not even empty space, with all the potential that implies, but absence, absence only. The nothing, the nowhere, the not-being-here. (*M.* p.137)

Gabriel finds peace when he is in contact with the machine; it communicates with him; it has its own "voices" and becomes equated with the voice of his own pain, as *"infinity was still infinity, zero still gaped, voracious as ever"*. The state of maximum entropy ("thermal death" is when there is no more energy exchange) that appears in irreversible processes, is equivalent to zero due to the strength of Gabriel's pain. However, after experiencing chaos in the bar on the mountain where drug addicts lose all notion of space and time fighting against each other, Gabriel is enlightened with a revelation of order within chaos, of a synthesis that contemplates determinism and chance:

> Something surged within me, yearning outwards into the darkness. And all at once I saw again clearly the secret I had lost sight of for so long, that chaos is nothing but an infinite number of ordered things. Wind, those stars, that water falling on stones, all the shifting, ramshackle world could be solved. (...) I lingered on the dark road, drunk on the knowledge of the

secret order of things. The wind swirled, the stars trembled. I seemed to fall upwards, into the night. (*M.*, pp.3-184)

There is nothing that is not part of the whole. He knows this "truth" quite well; the difference lies in the fact that numbers do not represent the "soul" of the things, they are only *"a method, a way of doing"*. The subtlety of things is Copernicus's transcendental questioning. Dr. Kasperl's black notebook irritates Gabriel due to its contradictions and paradoxes:

> Why should I worry about the nature of irrational numbers, or addle my brain any longer with the puzzle of what in reality a negative quantity could possibly be? Zero is absence. Infinity is where impossibilities occur. (*M.*, p.186)

Zero is not nothingness any more, it neither becomes absolute absence nor original chance. There is an implicit order in chaos. The machine once again becomes the symbol of harmony in numbers: *"The machine sang to me, for was not I too built on a binary code? One and zero, these were the poles"* (202).

Being and absence! Professor Kosok insists on the idea that anyone seeking order must invent it. According to Felix, the aim of the professor's work is to prove that nothing can be proved: *"O world in chaos! he intoned. Blind energy, spinning in the void! All turns, returns. Thus spake the prophet"* (226).

According to the principles of contemporary Physics, evolution is controlled by the principle of uncertainty. Chance is a constituent of nature and we have access to a series of probabilities rather than certainties. Gabriel's mistake is that he uses pluralities as unities in order to verify how they behave, instead of defining the law of relativity in relation to the simultaneity of distant facts while trying to understand their evolution. He tries to apply algebraic formulae to the world without success:

> I rummaged through the recent past, looking for the patterns that I must have missed. But, as once with numbers, so now with events, when I dismantled them they became not simplified, but scattered, and the more I knew, the less I seemed to understand. (*M.*, p. 187)

The search for synthesis in the realm of numbers is doomed to failure!:

> One drop of water plus one drop of water will not make two drops, but one. Two oranges and two apples do not make four of some new synthesis, but remain stubbornly themselves. (...) About numbers I had known everything, and understood nothing. (*M.*, p.233)

Just as Copernicus and Kepler experience revelation on their death-bed, so Gabriel is redeemed through original chance and decides to go back to the beginning, to the simplest things, in order to be different and to leave everything to chance: *"I won't do as I used to, in the old days. No. In the future, I will leave things, I will try to leave things, to chance"* (233).

Banville closes his tetralogy by wondering, on a metafictional level, whether ends are tied up – *"even an invented world has its rules, tedious, absurd perhaps, but not to be gainsaid"*.

According to the writer, *Mefisto* is not a perfect novel; it is just one more step in the search for a new synthesis in fiction:

> Mefisto is full of strange pain and grief. . . . A lot of things got into it that I didn't understand, but I let them stay. The book caused me terrible problems because I finished it with the technical problems unsolved. I didn't get the tone, but I was very proud of having finished it in spite of not solving the problems.[69]

In *Mefisto*, Banville crosses the boundaries of Science, Philosophy and (meta)fiction, although he believes that it is dangerous to be seduced by ideas because their incarnation damages fiction, and vice-versa:

> I've always been seduced by them. There is a danger in that. You can't bring ideas into fiction and discuss them because the fiction damages the ideas and the ideas damage the fiction.[70]

---

[69] Fintan O'Toole, "Stepping into the limelight - and the chaos". In: *The Irish Times*, October 21, 1989.
[70] Ciaran Carty, "Out of Chaos Comes Order". In: *The Sunday Tribune*. 14 Sep. 1986. p.18

Nevertheless, he puts himself at risk as a novelist and works ideas out in his search for order and, when he fails to find it, he invents it, following Kosok and Gabriel's advice.

I believe that Banville nearly succeeds in applying the synthesis proposed by Prigogine and Stengers to *Mefisto*: the idea of order out of chaos. Without lamenting his past and while looking for a unifying thread between present and future, the narrator of *Mefisto* describes chaos, perceiving that chance is the motor that propels the infinite sequence of order/disorder along the "arrow of life".

For Banville, each book is the end of one stage and the beginning of another:

> That's why all novels fail. If you really thought it was just the end, you'd never write any more. Mefisto was even more so the beginning of a new phase I don't know anything about. I could see there was quite a difference between it and the previous three. The science element was very low in importance. It's more my farewell to science.[71]

Banville is more interested in shapes and forms rather than in stories. He finds in them an approximation to beauty. He says he likes *"all art to be cold and pure"* and *"Mathematics rightly viewed possesses not only truth but supreme beauty – a beauty cold and austere, like that of sculpture"*.[72] This statement coincides with Prigogine and Stengers's conception of the universe, which is expressed by a reference to sculpture where there is a clear search for *"a junction between stillness and motion, time arrested and time passing."* [73] The various kinds of chance described throughout *Mefisto* create the effect of a sculpture. Gabriel's suffering is frozen in words but keeps burning in the reader's mind when the writer amalgamates various philosophical ideas with science and relativizes them in a fictional discourse.

---

[71] *Ibid.*, pp.18-19.
[72] Lavinia Greacen, L. "A Serious Writer. Lavinia Greacen met Banville". In: *The Irish Times*, March 24, 1981. p.8.
[73] Ilya Prigogine & Isabelle Stengers. *Order out of chaos.* p.23.

The "Turning Point" in Literature

Throughout my analysis of the tetralogy I have stressed how Banville proposes to create an interaction between Literature, Science, History and Philosophy in order to break down the compartmentalised stagnation of human thought. The writer's proposal results in the creation of a conceptual system of argumentative strategies which makes use figures of speech which are traditionally only accepted in the literary field. Recent research has shown that the processes of human thought are highly metaphorical and independent of the field of action. If language is a means of communicating knowledge, we must see ourselves as the agents of a new dialogue between human beings and nature at a turning point in our hitherto accepted view of the world.

The human being exists within a context and establishes an interaction between his inner and outer worlds, having a systemic vision of the universe that cannot be interpreted through Cartesian science. Banville proposes a new perception of the real which respects the wisdom of nature and the dynamics of the self-organisation of human thought. In the last book of his tetralogy he depicts the temporary victory of chaos over apparent order because, as Rosset argues, it is necessary to recognise the "truth" that exists in chance. According to Banville, this is a temporal truth because it is itself another construction of the human mind charged with an ethical responsibility. The ideas of instability, fluctuation and irreversibility disclose the power of choice in the bifurcations of an individual life and how a person can alter the determinism of a globalizing system.

Banville believes that the "two cultures", science and literature, interact due to our need for change and creativity. Such interactions produce self-transformations in the cognitive system which is kept in delicate balance by means of chance. Scientists whose syntheses have brought about scientific revolutions have always advocated a return to simplicity. Such an attitude stands opposed to the materialistic culture which is typical of our capitalist and post-industrial society.

Copernicus's dilemma over appearance and reality, Kepler's instinctive intuition, Newton's crisis of absolute values, the theories of Einstein and his successors concerning the relativity of time and space, and the ways in which chaos and order are produced by chance, all reflect the necessity of interrogating reality as a construct. We can only know the laws governing phenomena and not their essence. Thus, Banville makes his appeal in Gabriel Swan's voice when he concludes in *Mefisto*, *"I will leave things, I will try to leave things, to chance"*. This idea quoted before, reminds me of a poem called "Instants", of unknown authorship and initially wrongly attributed to Borges, in which an eighty-five year old confesses that, if he could walk again along the roads of life, he would leave things more to chance. Although the poem is not his, Borges expresses the same desire many times. In an interview Banville gave to me, he said that he admires Borges's writing for the way he works out ideas, but the Irish writer insists that he "would like to give more life to them in his books".

The newly-born literature that crosses the frontiers of literature and interacts with other fields of knowledge, especially science, will also meet other forms of literature, and the point of intersection will be a "turning point",[74] governed by the need of context, time and chance. The resultant mutation will produce a new synthesis in the field of art. It will be the transformation of a stone into a masterpiece, capturing the temporal and the eternal, movement and stagnation, order and chaos, as Prigogine and Stengers proposed in their new scientific synthesis.

---

[74] Capra uses this term in his book *The Turning Point* to describe the beginning of a new culture.

Jan Vermeer of Delft, "Portrait of a Woman".
Museum of Fine Arts, Buda-Pesth

III

THE ART OF WRITING AND THE VISUAL ARTS

> I was at a turning point, you will tell me, just there the future forked for me, and I took the wrong path without noticing - that's what you'll tell me, isn't it, you, who must have meaning in everything, who lust after meaning, your palms sticky and your faces on fire! But calm, Frederick, calm. Forgive me this outburst, your honour. (*The Book of Evidence*, p.24)[1]

The Labyrinth of Multiplicity

Having deconstructed the problems of the construction of an identity and the divided self in his first two novels, *Nightspawn* and *Birchwood*, and the question of order and truth within chaos in his tetralogy, Banville went on to write a trilogy - *The Book of Evidence* (1989), *Ghosts* (1993) and *Athena* (1995) - in order to analyse the multiplicity of selves, multiple possibilities, and ways in which chaos within the apparent order of human behaviour subverts our assumptions concerning the authentic and the real.

These questions seem to be at variance with Banville's idea, expressed in "Physics and Fiction: Order from Chaos", that within the human being there is *"a separate reality, which has shape and significance ... and which is endowed with*

---

[1] John Banville, *The Book of Evidence*. London: Secker & Warburg, 1989. All quotations refer to this edition.

a beginning, a middle and an end".[2] But this idea in fact supplements the others, as I mentioned in the introduction and in the analysis of the tetralogy that the systems of non-equilibrium are sources of order.

In his trilogy, Banville rewrites the life of Freddie Montgomery from various angles as though it were a "hologram" of the human universe, an image created by the mind which contains both matter and conscience as if they had been fused into a single field.

In *The Holographic Universe,* Michael Talbot explains a new concept of reality inspired by the principle of holography (the tridimensional reproduction of images by laser), according to which the universe is a huge hologram, whose image subverts the ideas of classical science, which considered the system as a whole, the result of the interaction of its parts. According to the holographic principle, the behaviour of the parts is organised by the whole. The parts act as integrated totalities, where time and space disappear, generating the principle of "non-locality". This holographic model influenced research in the field of Psychology and produced a revolution in the interpretation of human behaviour because, despite appearances, there are no frontiers and human consciousness is interrelated. Michael Talbot says that this concept recalls the collective unconscious of Carl Jung.[3] Recognising that things are component parts of an indivisible totality and yet retain their individual unique qualities, the physicist David Bohm, instead of calling the various aspects of a holomovement *"things",* describes them as *"relatively independent subtotalities"* [4] to demonstrate that, despite their differences, they make a collective sense. Analogically, Banville explores the fragments comprising the narrator's micro-cosmos which represents an indivisible whole (the human being) which nonetheless has unique qualities. The trilogy reveals how Freddie creates an abstraction out of the waves, eddies

---

[2] In: *The New York Times Book Review,* April 21, 1985, p.41.
[3] Michael Talbot, (1991) *The Holographic Universe.* Trans. Maria de Fátima S.M. Marques. *O Universo Holográfico.* Editora Nova Cultural. p.83.
[4] *Ibid.,* p.73.

and whirlpools of the river of his life to bring perception to its highest extreme, enabling him to develop a new way of thought and writing in the literary field.

A "necessary" fact that occurs at the different bifurcations of life is revisited in the three novels to reveal the vortexes of the mind and the multiple personalities of the narrator's self, either silenced or uncontrollable and rebellious, though all of them share a unique, indivisible being. The fact in question is the information that Freddie, an ex-academic, had murdered a young maid who discovered him as he was robbing an eighteenth-century Dutch painting from a friend's house.

In Imhof's review of *Ghosts,* he affirms that *"if **The Book of Evidence** is, to a large extent, about the world as perceived by the artistic imagination, then* Ghosts *is about the world as **created** by the artistic imagination".*[5] Following this train of thought I would add that *Athena* closes the trilogy as an example of such aesthetic explanations of this world.

In the first book, *The Book of Evidence,* Freddie who studied science at university (recalling the tetralogy), writes a self-defence in reverse, which he addresses to the judge and jury, narrating a pseudo-autobiography and giving significance or not to each of his transgressions in order to discover the essence of his criminal act – a motive for the crime. The narrator paints with well-defined brushstrokes the dramatic chiaroscuro of his thoughts and ideas, in the flux and reflux of his conscience, imitating the strokes of the "anonymous" painter of the stolen picture, which he abandoned in a ditch after he had killed the woman with a hammer.

> What was I thinking of, I don't know. Perhaps it was a gesture of renunciation or something. Renunciation! How do I dare use such words. The woman with the gloves gave me a last, dismissive stare. She had expected no better of me. (*T.B.E.*, p.119)

The historical doubt concerning the authorship of the picture – *Portrait of a Woman with Gloves* - which was first attributed to Rembrandt and then to Frans

---

[5] *ABEI Newsletter* No.8, August 1994. p.8.

Hals, before finally being proved to be by Vermeer, moves Banville to question, in an analogous way, the authorship of his character's crime due to his multiple selves. Freddie reveals the multiplicity of his self to the court many times, and he points out that the essence of his crime is his incapacity to impede the actions of those of his numerous selves that believe that *"nothing was forbidden, that everything was possible."*[6] In this way he demonstrates the fragility of the thesis that argues that moral culpability exists when free will is ambiguously absent:

> I had done the things I did because I could do no other. (...) I am merely asking, with all respect, whether it is feasible to hold on to the principle of moral culpability once the notion of free will has been abandoned. (*T.B.E.*, p. 16).

Freddie also questions the authenticity of those who wear masks and are true actors on the world's stage. This stereotyped vision of the world, which is already a *cliché* in the field of literature, will be the narrator's target in the process of desacralization during his trial:

> ... I should live henceforth among actors, practise among them, study their craft, the grand gesture and the fine nuance. Perhaps in time I would learn to play my part sufficiently well, with enough conviction, to take my place among the others, the naturals, those people on the bus, and all the rest of them. (*T.B.E.*, p.133)

At the end of the trial he unmasks its very "authenticity". When he was offered a trial without evidence, Freddie refuses to accept the prearranged sentence according to the ritual of the Court of Justice. Although he is guilty, his lawyer asks him to deny the crime and not to sign any confession. He has to collaborate, waiting for the right moment to plead guilty to the charge of murder. The rules of the game dictate that the lawyer's duty is to guarantee his client the best judgement possible. Freddie cannot accept this game of appearances because he can only perceive the essence of the crime and the significance of having abandoned the stolen picture in a ditch as evidence:

---

[6] *The Book of Evidence*, p.151.

How could mere facts compare with the amazing knowledge that had flared out at me as I stood and stared at the painting lying on its edge in the ditch where I dropped it that last time? That knowledge, that knowingness, I could not have lived with. (*T.B.E.* p. 214)

The object of the robbery, Johannes Vermeer's work of art, is as self-sufficient, complete and enigmatic as Banville's self-contained work. Each element of the Dutch artist's pictorial style forms a continuum and reveals fragments of his thoughts and feelings related to his everyday life. Freddie rewrites his "defence" following both the evidential and, above all, the non-evidential trials because, when everyday details are exploded into atoms, even if non-evidential, they contain the whole in a holographic form and become condemning *evidence* in his final trial. When the Inspector receives the written confession from Freddie's hands, in order to keep it together with the other "official fictions", he asks him indirectly how much of it is true. Freddie concludes his narrative by saying, *"True, Inspector? I said. All of it. None of it. Only the shame"* (220)..

As if he were dividing his canvas into logical spaces, Banville firmly outlines the central story in the first book of the trilogy. Each field is painted in warm Rembrandt's rich and earthy colours and delimited with Vermeer's delicate brushstrokes to give texture to the images he is portraying throughout his narrative. The presence of a beam of light coming from an angle produces shadows that interrupt and deny the existence of defined lines and project themselves onto the portrayed person from one side. The limits become blurred and disappear into the background of the canvas in an impressionistic way, though as the result of techniques different from those that gave their name to that school of painting. Banville uses a deconstructive technique, reversing the beam of light and focusing on the dark side of the human face and of the art of writing. In this way he produces a questioning shadow on the face of what was previously visible. This dislocation reveals in an ironic way that the essential sin in the crime was the murderer's lack of imagination: he did not conceive of the young woman as being alive!

> I killed her because I could kill her, and I could kill her because for me she was not alive. And so my task now is to bring her back to life. I am not sure what that means, but it strikes me with the force of an unavoidable imperative. How am I to make it come about, this act of parturition? Must I imagine her from the start, from infancy? I am puzzled, and not a little fearful, and yet there is something stirring in me, and I am strangely excited. I seem to have taken on a new weight and density. I feel gay and at the same time wonderfully serious. I am big with possibilities. I am living for two. (*T.B.E.*, p.216)

Throughout the trilogy, Freddie attempts to transform death into life as he did with the stolen portrait when he saw it for the first time: his imagination breathed life into it and he felt seduced by the look of the young woman portrayed on the canvas. He confirms this in the following book *Ghosts:*

> Let us take the hypothetical case of a man surprised by love, not for a living woman - he has never been able to care much for the living - but for the figure of a woman in, oh, a painting, let's say. That is, he is swept off his feet one day by a work of art. It happens; not very often, I grant you, but it does happen. (*G.*, pp. 83-84)

The portrait is evidence of the crime – it acquires life while the maid, who discovered him robbing it, has none because she is an external element in the interactive act that occurs between the observer and the observed. Freddie describes the stolen picture to the jury and he becomes apparently distracted into describing the effect of the painted lady's stare, thus giving life to the invisible that lies behind its non-locality and atemporality:

> I stood there, staring for what seemed a long time, and gradually a kind of embarrassment took hold of me, a hot, shamefaced awareness of myself, as if somehow I, this soiled sack of flesh, were the one who was being scrutinised, with careful, cold attention. It was not just the woman's painted stare that watched me. Everything in the picture, that brooch, those gloves, the flocculent darkness at her back, every spot on the canvas was an eye fixed on me unblinkingly. I retreated a pace, faintly aghast. (*T.B.E.*, p.79)

There is a distancing and defamiliarization in the act of sublimation of the work of art. The observer is held by the woman's stare and lives out the processes of incorporation and reconciliation with her with the aid of perception. To look is an act of choice and the way things are seen depends on the viewer's previous knowledge and beliefs. Banville therefore emphasises the interaction between observer and observed, pointing out the reciprocal nature of vision: our own eye interacts with the eye of the other in order to authorise the presence of both in the visible world. Freddie's experience, which reveals an altered state of consciousness, transcends the ordinary frontiers of personality. It is a transpersonal experience that is introduced to the jury and the reader-listener as a hologram containing an enormous amount of information not only about the accused but also about the awakening of aesthetic perception. The boundaries become illusory and there is no distinction between the parts and the whole. Each part is the whole and produces a terrifying effect when he experiences the union of all things without spatial or temporal limits. The image is a recreated or reproduced figure; it is an appearance that makes the absent material, present but ignored, and the perception of that image depends directly on the way of seeing. The image-maker becomes part of the image, conscious of his individuality as its constructor. Freddie's visible experience of the essence of art is when the texture of paint reveals a saturation in the act of perceiving the fragments - unique totalities. As he has no words to describe it, he is cast loose from the mooring-ropes of the mind. The illusion of the artist holding the power of style to imprison reality is destroyed by Vermeer who, according to Lawrence Gowing,[7] believed that light is the only thing that the eye can capture and that this fact establishes an emotional equilibrium. Banville demystifies the same illusion in the field of words because they rarely signify what they seem to represent – *"Words so rarely mean what they mean"*:

---

[7] Lawrence Gowing, *Vermeer*. London: Faber & Faber. n.d.

> Ever since I had reached what they call the use of reason I had been doing one thing and thinking another, because the weight of things seemed so much greater than that of thoughts. What I said was never exactly what I felt, what I felt was never what it seemed I should feel, though the feelings were what felt
> genuine, and right, and inescapable. (*T.B.E.*, p.124)

The focus of the narrator is the same as that of Vermeer, everyday life and its routine. The jury is not interested in the common facts of everyday life because they are non-evidential, but their details demonstrate the presence of evidence: the dark side of the human being which is uncontrollable and ignored because of its multiplicity and fear of the unknown. He felt himself trapped inside a body not his own, "*I say the one within was strange to me, but which version of me do I mean? No, not clear at all. But it was not a new sensation, I have always felt - what is the word - bifurcate, that's it*" (95).

Freddie is aware of the vortices of his structured thought and interacts with the multiple fragments of his self, making way for the flux of the order implicit within chaos. In the non-evidential, holographic trial in which he pleads guilty, he presents these minor totalities as self-sustained and complete, fully conscious that they are evidence. The narrative swings between a holographic self and other selves, provoking a pendulum motion that reflects global, physiological and psychological changes. According to him, the essence of his crime is that he was not vigilant enough and let the monster inside come out. "*He is me, after all, and I am he.*" (151)

Freddie analyses all his acts rationally from a perspective irreversible in its completeness, opening the way towards the presence of the non-existent: the ghost of the human being, the other self "in the wings". When he narrates the facts prior to the robbery, particularly the purchase of the hammer, he confesses the existence of the ghost of his childhood that lies beneath the shadow of his other self:

> But I insist, your honour, gentle handymen of the jury, I insist it was an innocent desire, a wish, an ache, on the part of the deprived child inside me - not Bunter, not him, but the true, lost ghost of my boyhood - to possess this marvellous toy. (*T.B.E*, p. 97)

The ghosts of his multiple selves are present throughout the trilogy and become the central theme of the second book, *Ghosts*. In "Survivors of Joyce",[8] Banville refers to the meaning Nietzsche gave to the word ghost in order to show how Irish writers must live with the ghost of the great master, which is like an invented human being striving to signify something necessary for the comprehension of the whole. Thus, Freddie's ghosts appear in the voice of the anonymous narrator, who is also one of his multiple selves, " *there is an onus on us, the living, to conjure up our particular dead. . . . they should live in us, and through us* (83). He also adds that, even if the ghosts of the past are our burden, they do not have to feed our fear because it is through them that it is possible to understand the present and the future. In this way, Banville rewrites the main theme of *The Book of Evidence*, transforming each image of the past into ghosts which, instead of tormenting him, help him to comprehend better not only the intimacy of the human being but also the process of writing a novel.

Ghost is a fictional autobiographical narrative which describes a day in the life of a group of people who are shipwrecked on the coast of the island where Freddie Montgomery was living after having served his prison sentence. This group is analogous to that depicted in a painting by the fictional artist Jean Vaublin which is described by the narrator many times throughout his narrative. The group occupies the house of Professor Kreutznaer for some hours while they are awaiting high tide in order to be rescued. Banville outlines on his canvas Freddie's revisited past, using the technique used by the eighteenth-century French painter Jean-Antoine Watteau (Vaublin in fiction) in his portrait of the dramatic *Gilles* in the context of the *commedia dell'arte*. In *Pierrot-Watteau: A*

---

[8] In: Augustine Martin (ed.), *James Joyce: The artist and the Labyrinth*. London: Ryan, 1990. pp.73-81.

Nineteenth-Century Myth, Louisa Jones analyses Watteau's pictures highlighting some of the characteristics that helped to model my analysis of *Ghosts*. The infinite number of view-points of the same observed object, its representation and reception, the portrayal of absences, the fragmented studies as preparatory designs for later pictures with mythological or historical themes, the rich visual vocabulary typical of the *Rococo,* the moment captured and transformed into durability, are all reproduced in the field of words, not only in the theme but also on the discursive level.

Ghosts is a portrait of the static in movement – the completed irreversible past becoming alive in the present – and vice-versa, the living captured and frozen by the eye. The different points of view of the portrayed object – e.g. the overlapping of Vaublin's work of art with the fictional recreation of the crime and its victim – are the fragmented study of the real that will become part of more complete pictures in *Athena*. Banville follows the principle of perspective where everything is centralized upon the point of view of the observer and the evanescent point of the infinite. The observer loses his substantiality and resembles the ghosts of his multiple selves:

> For I felt like something suspended in empty air, weightless, transparent, turning this way or that in every buffet of wind that blew. At least when I was locked away I had felt I was definitively there, but now that I was free (or at large, at any rate) I seemed hardly to be here at all. This is how I imagine ghosts existing, poor, pale wraiths pegged out to shiver in the wind of the world like so much insubstantial laundry, yearning towards us, the heedless ones, as we walk blithely through them. (*G.*, p. 37)

The same sense of immanence that elevates him to the quality of a phantom, of being *"a patch of moving dark against the lighter darkness"* (p.38), also allows him to retain his shrewd perception and review his crime numerous times seeking its essence and the rebirth of the victim:

> And how, having done away with her, was he to bring her back? For that, he understood, was his task now. Prison, punishment, paying his debt to

society, all that was nothing, was merely how he would pass the time while he got on with the real business of atonement, which was nothing less than the restitution of a life. Restitution, that was the word, he remembered it from when he was a child at school and they told him what the thief must do, which is to make proper restitution. (*G.*, p. 86)

He refers to himself as a "hypothetical man" and he asks himself from a distance if, in the multiplicity of worlds, *"in this infinite mirrored regression"*, it is possible for the dead not to die and for him to become innocent. As time is not reversible all that he can do is to conjure up the presence of the ghost of the victim, to hear the voices of the dead and to live in the shadows waiting for a new point of access to life, for a new bifurcation and choice. His "true" and innocent self becomes unprotected when it is seduced by the work of art. As chance rules time, Freddie is overcome by his monstrous multiple self and he suffers an eternal return to the dark side of human beings on both levels, that of the story and that of the narrative discourse.

All the questionings of *The Book of Evidence* are revisited and recreated: the actors and their masks, multiplicity, chaos and chance, the past in the present – *"How the present feeds on the past, or versions of the past"* – the voice of the unconscious in dreams and their multiple meanings, and the question of authenticity. Freddie's burden is his aimless liberty which anticipates his phantasmagoric future – the reflection of the image of Watteau's Gilles:

> Forget the past, then, give up all hope of retrieving my lost selves, just let it go, just let it all fall away? And then be something new, a sticky, staggering thing with myriad-faceted eyes and wet wings, an astonishment standing up in the world, straining drunkenly for flight. Was that it, that I must imagine myself into existence before tackling the harder task of conjuring another? (*G.*, pp.195-96)

Banville divides the second book of the trilogy into four parts of different length with a non-narrative. The first part occupies a wider space and focalises each shipwrecked person. They wait for rescue lost in their thoughts and their fears appear in flashes because they perceive unconsciously that they have already been

Antoine Watteau, "Gilles".

Musée du Louvre.

In: Herausgegeben von E. Heinrich Zimmermann, *Watteau*. Stuttgart & Leipzig, Deutsche Verlags Anstalt, 1912.

in that place in the past. They are the personification of the characters that appear upstage in the painting *Gilles*, recreated in Flora's dream: Felix (an echo of *Mefisto*) is the doctor riding a donkey on the left of the canvas; she recognises Litch, the professor's assistant, inside the stuffed animal; the juxtaposition of Flora and Sophie, the famous photographer who captures images of still life, resembles the young actress; the older man is Croke and the other is the captain. The three children and Sophie overlap in the dream but they are also the models for other pictures mentioned in the narrative. Gilles, *"the childish man, the mannish child"*, is the narrator. His enormous and deformed image, clothed in white and portrayed as though he were suspended in mid-air, evokes his own phantom. The mask with its slight smile conceals his tragedy which surpasses the *commedia dell'arte*. The *troupe* activates the narrator's phantoms, which in their turn evoke the past chaotically; however, he distances himself when he recreates his past aesthetically, defining himself as a *"hypothetical man"*. The narrator's thoughts occupy the centre of the written portrait, forming multiple versions and maelstroms. The question of authenticity is also discussed, along with that of the presence of ghosts: at the end of his life, Vaublin advocates the existence of a ghost, his double, who knows every detail of his technique and reproduces not only his most perfect drawing lines but also his faults. The double recalls in the mind of the narrator the professor's past and his fraud, arousing a doubt as to whether he himself was the double who had produced the paintings with the same lines as the painter.

The second part is a flashback that introduces the reader to the moment when Freddie leaves prison and has his first contact with the exterior world in which there is apparent order though, in fact, all is chaos and chance: *"In this manifold version of reality chance is an iron law. Chance. Think of it."* (173)

Freddie's beginning of a new life on an island, *"Cythera"* – a clear reference to another of Watteau's pictures – is aimed at self-exiling his multiple selves. Anna Behrens (the owner of the Vermeer which was the object of his crime in *The Book of Evidence* and the inauthenticity of which was the probable cause for his abandoning it in the ditch after having killed the maid) recommends him to Professor Kreutznaer. The professor is a famous specialist in eighteenth-century art who lives in isolation on the island with his assistant Licht, having unfortunately authenticated as Vaublin's some false paintings, and who devotes himself to writing about the painter's work. However, the narrator's exile is not sufficient to free him from the shadows that produce the dislocation of the self and torment him:

> It is as if mind and body had pulled loose from each other, or as if the absolute, essential I had shrunk to the size of a dot, leaving the rest of me hanging in enormous suspension, massive and yet weightless, like a sawn tree before it topples. (*G.*, p.176)

The fragmentation of the self and an atomised perception of reality do not prevent the essence of the whole from continuing in each atom, as occurs with the holographic image. The narrator identifies himself with just such an image when he enters his empty house after leaving prison: "*I say myself as if lit by lightning, a stark, crouched figure, vivid and yet not entirely real, an emanation of myself, a hologram image, pop-eyed and flickering*" (179).

Banville gives shape to space, showing the fragment not only as a part of the whole but also as the very image of the whole when apprehended in its original form. The reader also discovers that the writer is reproducing Watteau's style when he portrays the absences and ends of the episodes, making them disappear into the infinite and showing his interest in the performatic quality of everyday life. The narrator rediscovers Diderot's philosophical painting principles, one of which states that the human being is an actor who is portraying himself in order to survive in the multitude:

> And there I was all that time thinking it was others I must imagine into life. Well well. (To act is to be, to rehearse is to become: Felix dixit, or someone like him.) This has the feel of a great discovery. I'm sure it must be a delusion. (*G.*, pp.198-99)

When Freddie enters his mother's house, looking for his belongings, he stumbles upon the presence of his own absence and silence: *"I could touch nothing, could not feel the texture of things: the house had been emptied of me; I had been exorcised from it"* (180). The narrator multiplies himself and becomes aware of his own self transformed into his own phantom:

> I closed my eyes and was assailed anew by that feeling of both being and not being, of having drifted loose from myself. I have always been convinced of the existence somewhere of another me, my more solid self, more weighty and far more serious than I, intent perhaps on great and unimaginable tasks, in another reality, where things are really real; ... (*G.*, p.181)

In the future he will have another house, and another search for God – the Great Nought – impelling him to action. On the island, each person in the house becomes part of an implicit ceremony, whose apparent paradigms become dissolved with time and transformed into new ones: *"things shift suddenly, the whole pattern falling apart and reassembling itself in a new way out of the old pieces"* (219).

The third part of the novel consists of a critical description of the painting itself. Banville uses the artist's technique of placing the figures together, in pairs, and mutually absorbed, just the opposite of Vermeer's painting in which the introspection of the character pushes the observer to the centre of the maelstrom as a result of the act of looking. Watteau's figures rarely face the observer, though when they do look at him they reveal themselves to be actors of the Italian *commedia dell'arte*: the Venetian merchant Pantalone, Isabella and Horacio the disappointed lovers, the young and mischievious servant Harlequim, the musician Mezetino and the innocent Pierrot or Gilles. The artist uses everyday reality and represents life converted into art in the same way as it is transformed on stage. Moreover, he raises Gilles to the status of a hero for the first time, placing him in the centre of the canvas in an abnormal size. The figure generates the expectation of an event which is linked to feelings that are never translated into action. When the narrator describes him, he traces a parallel to his own personality, personifying him as if he were a ghost:

> He stands before us like our own reflection distorted in a mirror, known yet strange. What is he doing here, on this raised ground, in this gilded, inexplicable light? He is isolated from the rest of the figures ranged behind him, suspended between their world and ours, a man alone. Has he dropped from the sky or risen from the underworld? We have the sense of a mournful apotheosis. (*G.* p.225)

His image is associated with the phantasmagoric past of the narrator and he suspects him as though he had also committed a terrible crime: *"What is it he has done, what crime is he guilty of? And from whom is he hiding, if he is hiding?"* (228).

The four-page description of the painting attempts to define the origin and essence of each character and ends in a speculation: nothing matters, whether it portrays the artists of the *Comedie Française* or the painter's friends in their disguises. What is valid is the moment caught by the artist's eye.

In the last part of the novel, the narrator tries to return to a non-existent plot. The troupe returns to the boat as represented in the middle ground of the picture. Flora stays at the house for some time but she will also leave the place. The authenticity of Vaublin/Watteau's painting continues in the dark and the theme returns to the referent, the end of the first part where, as in *Athena*, the authenticity of the pictures that the professor is studying is questioned. The painter's double becomes his own shadow rather than an impostor or plagiarist as occurs with the idea of true-false. Banville ends his novel with certainty generated by the doubt as to whether the picture is a fake or not:

> My writing is almost done: Vaublin shall live! If you call this life. He too was no more than a copy, of his own self. As I am, of mine.
> No: no riddance. (*G.*, p. 245)

The authenticity of the picture is not only questioned. The true name of the fictional painter produces alternatives that refer to a chaotic game of letters which may be recomposed into the name John Banville *("Faubelin, Vanhoblin, Van Hobellijn?")*.[9] These names of fictional painters appear as authors of various paintings of mythical themes in *Athena*, demonstrating how Banville's narrative technique mirrors Watteau's pictorial technique: the fragments are studies that will become the whole in future pictures.

Athena is the last novel in the trilogy, and has the same narrator, Freddie Montgomery, but this time using a fictional name, Mr. Morrow: *"I chose it for its faintly hopeful hint of futurity, and, of course, the Wellsian echo"* (7).

Freddie feels the need to look for a new identity in the hope of finding a new way of life. Banville begins and ends his novel as in *The Newton Letter*, in the form of a letter addressed to a lost love aimed at reviewing the past and understanding the lack of any feeling of loss in the present - writing for its own sake - *"Write to me, she said. Write to me. I have written."* These are the words that end the novel.

The narrator has a contract, as a specialist in eighteenth-century art, to analyse the authenticity of seven oil paintings: *Pursuit of Daphne* ca. 1680 by Johann Livelb (1633-1697); *The Rape of Proserpine* 1655 by L. van Hobelijn (1608-1674); *Pygmalion (called Pygmalion and Galatea)* 1649 by Giovanni Belli (1602-1670); *Syrinx Delivered* 1645 by Job van Hellin (1598-1647); *Capture of Ganymede* 1620 by L.E. van Ohlbijn (1573-1621); *Revenge of Diana* 1642 by J. van Hollbein (1595-1678); *Acis and Galatea* 1677 by Jan Vibell (1630-1690). In my opinion, the themes of the pictures introduce the action of the narrated events, showing that human actions are a repetition of universal archetypes that point back to the myths and return to Jung's idea of the collective unconscious. Banville re-writes the theme of *The Book of Evidence* and *Ghosts*, using the mythical connotations of the goddess of war, Athena, defender of the state and home

---

[9] In the manuscript of *Birchwood*, one can observe how Banville plays with the letters of his own

against external enemies, but this time based on Jungian concepts to demonstrate explicative alternatives for his story and for his vision of the theory of the novel.

In spite of the fact that Morrow has changed his name, the people around him know his past and use it to serve their own interests: Morden and Francie to study the eighteenth-century paintings, Da to sell them, Inspector Hackett to solve the crime, the young girl he calls *"A. My alpha; my omega"* to find masochistic sexual pleasure. The narrator's work is dubious and the narrative has two coincidental foci showing an unexpected synchronicity: an ill aunt close to death and his amorous relationship with the young woman which reawakens his potentiality as a murderer. The narrative consists of roads that bifurcate again and again to enable free will to produce a new questioning, not as something irreversible but as the reaffirmation of multiplicity and chance:

> We shall dispense with the disquisition on fate and the forked paths that destiny sets us upon and all such claptrap. There are no moments, only the seamless drift; how many times do I have to tell myself this simple truth?. . . No, what I mean simply is that I did not stop, did not turn aside, but went on, and so closed off all other possibilities . . . If there are other worlds in which the alternatives to our actions are played out we may know nothing of them. (*A.*, p.9)

Though there is a linearity in the structure of the work, this is interrupted by the description of the paintings of mythological subjects which continue the story by offering various possibilities of interpretation. Thus, actions are seen as the resonance of the myths that form the collective unconscious that is shared by everyone. In "Pursuit of Daphne", the horror and double despair seen in the eyes of Apollo and Daphne – partly because of the transformation of the girl into a tree but mainly because of the sense of loss of an object of desire and of human appearance – introduce a synchronism of the encounters between the narrator and his aunt, whose presence pursues him, and between the narrator and the young A., whom he pursues along the streets on the first day of his new job. The description

---

name when he is looking for an artistic name to be given to Gabriel.

of "The Rape of Proserpine" anticipates the relationship of the narrator with the young woman who will escort him to the border between life and death, revealing *"the frailty of human wishes and the tyrannical and irresistible force of destiny"*.

The act of rape is reversed in the two situations: A. invades his mind, inciting him to construct the rape in his thought first. In a parallel way, his secret from the past is violated by Morden and Francis who gave him the job of defining whether the pictures were authentic or not. This event produces a personal reflection on the feeling of culpability, having the picture *Gilles* as a referent:

> Guilt, I mean the permanent, inexpungible, lifetime variety, turns you into a kind of earnest clown. They speak of guilt as something heavy, they talk about the weight of it, the burden, but I know otherwise; guilt is lighter than air; it fills you up like a gas amd would send you sailing into the sky, arms and legs flailing, an inflated Grock, if you did not keep a tight hold on things. (*A.*, p.66)

In the same way that Pygmalion falls in love with his sculpture Galatea, to which Venus had given life, the narrator describes how A. acquires life for him - *"stepped out of your frame"*, with a magic touch - *"her face was unexpectedly cool under my hand"*, beginning a passionate physical relationship representing the theme of death or, more precisely, *"life-in-death"*. This situation brings the reader back to Freddie's aim in *The Book of Evidence*. The redemption of his crime can only occur if he gives life back to Rosie, the person he killed with a hammer. The urgent visit to his aunt in hospital places him at another crossroads made up of new possibilities: the people who are taking care of his Aunt Corky force him to construct another reality in his mind against his own will (that of taking his aunt to live with him), which would signify violating his individuality and, in order to preserve it, he has to lie:

> Amazing how the world keeps on offering new opportunities for betrayal. I thought I was finished with everything: desire and duty, compassion, the needs of others - in a word, life - yet here I was, mooning after a girl and lumbered with a dying relative, up to my oxters again in the whole bloody shenanigans. No wonder I was in a funk. (*A.*, p.96)

In "Syrinx Delivered", Pan is portrayed pursuing the nymph Syrinx madly while she hides among the reeds at the riverside and transfigures herself into the world of nature; the god perceives the mutation of his beloved and makes a flute out of the reed. According to the narrator she is the pivot of the picture, *"the representation of life-in-death and death-in-life, of what changes and yet endures"*, and of the possibility of transcending the self and the world while both remain the same. For the narrator, the past is always returning, and this time it does so in the persons of Inspector Hackett and A. They reactivate his lethargic memory, particularly when A. tells him that she is the survivor of twins – a reminiscence of *Mefisto,* which already has *Birchwood* as a referent, turning the narrative into an eternal return.

Just as the Trojan prince is captured by Zeus's eagle and taken to the Olympus in the painting "Capture of Ganymede", the narrator is captured in the web of synchronic events tied to chance: he is forced to take care of his aunt, to give a verdict upon the paintings, to participate in A.'s games, which become more and more dangerous due to their fantasy. There is culpability and impotence in all his transgressions because he cannot make his own choices:

> I did not know myself (do I ever know myself?). That is what home is for, to still the self's unanswerable questionings; now I had been invaded and the outer doubts were seeping in like fog through every fissure. (*A.*, p.149)

"Revenge of Diana" anticipates the triple death: the death of his relationship with A. when she reveals her need for sexual pleasure produced by the physical pain of whiplashes; Aunt Corky's death; the end of his job when he announces to Inspector Hackett that the paintings are genuine. The fear that the multiple selves could be reactivated, making all limits disappear, is present as though it were a phantom of himself.

> What if I broke something ('Go ahead, hit it!') and the trick did not work and it stayed broken? From some things there is no going back - who should know that better than I?. (*A.*, p.174)

The last picture, "Acis and Galatea", closes the narrative of the trilogy, anticipating that the narrator is Acis and Polyphemus in only one being, both victim and the murderous cyclops who will be united to his beloved in the triumph of transformation because the interior monster has been silenced:

> She had been mine for a time, and now she was gone. Gone, but alive, in whatever form life might have taken for her, and from the start that was supposed to be my task: to give her life. Come live in me, I had said, and be my love. (*A.*, p.223)

This victory is shown in the last chapter when the eighth painting that Dada wants to sell, "The Birth of Athena", is discovered by the police. This is a genuine painting that will be traded abroad in the middle of the seven fakes described at the beginning of each chapter. The last chapter represents a triple rebirth – the narrator's, free from sin; his beloved's, free from the danger of being killed; and that of the murdered maid, Rosie, who is reborn in him.

Echoes from *The Book of Evidence* and *Ghosts* – the crime, the masks, the phantoms, the individual as a multiple being, not a double one, the truth and the authentic, non-linearity – are contextualized holographically not only to demonstrate that the Jungean synchronies are real but also to offer further evidence for the existence of an implicit order. This fact refers back to the first concept that *Athena* is the explanation of the aesthetic world created by Banville in which order is born from chaos.

A Crossroads of Discourses

In this last part of my work the voices of the various critics of John Banville's work gradually disappear as the "arrow of time" nears the present. Few reviews of *Ghosts* have been published as critics have referred more to the previous books rather than to that novel, which reveals the hermetical nature of the book. Due to the geographical distance (Brazil-Ireland) I have had no access to any critical review of *Athena*. My analysis of the trilogy has therefore been based on a dialogue with other fields of knowledge which helped me to understand the two most recent books. The hidden face of the human being and the projection of shadows portrayed in *The Book of Evidence* are illuminated by the narrative during the development of the trilogy, whether in the case of the tragic-comic Gilles or of Athena in her triumphant birth. But, I wonder, what is the dark face of the theory of the novel that Banville is trying to illuminate when he is searching for a "new" synthesis?

The trilogy is an echo of the whole work of the writer, offering a kind of non-linear detective story in the first and last books, which recall the first novels of Banville, *Nightspawn* and *Birchwood*. In my opinion, *Ghosts* is the ethereal centre, the proper field to recreate and analyse the evidence, both on the level of the story and of the theory of the novel.

According to the writer in his article "Survivors of Joyce", he feels himself to be split in two by the shadow of the master: he is the reader *"kneeling speechless in filial admiration"* and also the writer *"gnawing his knuckles"* as a survivor.[10] For Banville, something has happened to the language in which fiction is written, *"a meanness of tone, a weariness, a wariness. The small voice is the one that is favoured by writers and reviewers alike"*. He believes that literary language acquires energy from common speech which allows him to conjure up a

---

[10]In: Augustine Martin (ed), *James Joyce: The Artist and the Labyrinth*. p.74.

representation of reality *"that will be dense and weighty enough to seem not word but world"*.[11]

Banville's conviction strengthens my thesis, which is based on the conception of literature as a social practice. In the same article he reaffirms:

> I hasten to emphasise that by language here I mean literary language, and I suppose, since I am a fiction writer, I am thinking mainly of prose. The difference between what comes out when the man speaks and the artist writes is not sufficiently well appreciated, by readers, or, indeed, in some cases, by writers. It is an essential difference, as anyone who has ever written an essay, or a love letter, should know. Even the most colloquial-sounding piece of written prose will have been shaped by the action of laws that do not hold in the slip and slide, the dash and hesitancies of common speech.

He does not refer to *slang*, he prefers *"the rhythm of collective consciousness itself, which beats at the heart of talk"*.[12]

If his previous books were already not only intertextual but also an interaction between the discourses of the scientists and the contemporary discourses of the writer, whether fictional or not, the trilogy additionally reveals the interaction between the differences of the Fine Arts (verbal expression which uses arbitrary and conventional signs and pictorial expression which uses images of natural signs) and the interaction of representative discourses of different social practices.

In *The Book of the Evidence,* there is a reversion of legal discourse, and justice and truth themselves become the objects of analysis. In *Ghosts,* the limits between dreams and reality are surpassed; the predominant discourse and tone are surrealist due to the transformation of reality from a relative to an absolute quality. This surrealism activates thought in the absence of any rational and moral control. Thought is deconstructed in *Athena* by means of myths, not to give solutions but to offer possible perceptional alternatives that might explain the lack of limits between madness and non-madness, between life and death, the real and

---

[11] John Banville, "In the beginning were the words". In: Weekend Guardian. July 7-8, 1990. 20.
[12] *Ibid.*, p.20

the imaginary, past and future, the communicable and the incommunicable, high and low, without succumbing either to the absurdity of contradictions or to the oppositions of structuralism.

In order to give meaning for his art, Banville explores the institutionalised discourses of society, deconstructing the assumptions of the various professional areas, particularly where fossilised meanings have become absolutes and unquestionable in their use because they are the mirror of sacramental values.

Thus, in the first book of the trilogy, Banville subverts the function that the argumentative discourse of the defence has in a juridical process. He gives a voice to the defendant, who uses a highly persuasive discourse to convince the jury that he should be condemned. He is thus opposed to that defensive discourse which argues for a verdict of absolution, even when the convict declares himself to be guilty:

> . . . I was determining the course of my own life, according to my own decisions, but gradually, as I accumulated more and more past to look back on, I realised that I had done the things I did because I could do no other. Please, do not imagine, my lord, I hasten to say it, do not imagine that you detect here the insinuation of an apologia, or even of a defence. I wish to claim full responsibility of my actions - after all, they are the only things I can call my own - and I declare in advance that I shall accept without demur the verdict of the court. (*T.B.E.* p.16)

He calls his imaginary witnesses – his wife, his mother, the Inspector who loves details, his neglectful father, the taxi driver and his mother, and his friend Charlie – and he interprets his attitudes and relationship with them in a highly selective way, revealing the illusory character of the revelation or confession of truth within a legal trial. If the truth is constructed based on the existing laws, whose foundations are the values and assumptions of a particular social group, the final verdict will depend directly on those who judge that truth. In her comparative study of scientific and the legal discourse, Maria José Coracini confirms that *"the final verdict depends mainly on the cognitive structure of the jury, i.e. the way each member of the jury structures the data of evidence, combining and relating it* to themselves and their own viewpoints, knowledge and previous experience, which are permanently inseparable from any interpretative act".[13] This is the reason why the narrator ironises the *cliché* "to swear an oath to tell the truth, the whole truth and nothing but the truth". A sarcastic laugh is his answer to this oath: *"Don't make me laugh"*.

Banville deconstructs the symbol of justice, the perfect balanced scales, as being the social practice of an institution created by Man. According to a dictionary definition, the verdict (from the Latin: *verus+dictum = truth saying)* is a "decision of the jury made after judging the facts that are given, esp. one made at the end of the trial". The constituted significance connotes not only a "true" fact but also something "that is taken as true" by the sanction of the norm of a group of people who share elements of the same interpretative community. This is why truth and justice are relative if Coracini's statement is accepted.

The narrator of *The Book of Evidence,* as implied by the title, manipulates the information directly related to the crime, the *evidential,* and he interrelates it with *non-evidential* facts which explain not only his acts but also his thoughts. The narrative of highly logical reasoning shows spontaneous argument, either in formal or informal situations, inducing the jury to arrive at a "just" judgement: a unanimous verdict of guilty.

In the discourse of *Ghosts*, the intangible is caught by the imagination, resulting in a fusion between action and the static, reason and feelings, pointing out the various possibilities of discourse that interact on the physical, subjective and aesthetic levels. The text-image relationship stimulates Banville to translate pictorial discourse and technique into words:

> I live among ghosts and absences. A nightbird flies past, I hear the rapid whirr of wings, and down in the direction of the stream suddenly something gallops away. A horse? There are no horses here. A donkey, perhaps. I hear

---

[13]Maria José Coracini. *Um Fazer Persuasivo. O Discurso Subjetivo da Ciência.* São Paulo: Pontes & EDUC, 1991. p.54.

> it, clear as anything, the unmistakable sound of hoofbeats. Who is the horseman?
> Life, life: being outside.
> Night and silence and
> Oh life!
> And I in flames. (*G.*, p.73)

Watteau's Giles is grasped in its visibility, as the reproduction of an image, and in its invisibility, in the field of ideas and feelings. In "Going too far with the Sister Arts", W. J. Mitchell affirms that poetry is an art of time, motion and actions, while painting is an art of space, stasis and arrested action.[14]

Banville tries to capture a new synthesis with words when he blends action with the static, which is the principal characteristic of beauty in sculpture, just as Prigogine and Stengers define their scientific synthesis in *Order Out of Chaos*. The narrator also analyses the ethical theory developed by Diderot based on the idea of sculpture. Thus, it can be seen how Banville transforms the discourses of various areas of knowledge into an aesthetic discourse:

> if we would be good, he said, we must become sculptors of the self. Virtue is not natural to us; we achieve it, if at all, through a kind of artistic striving, cutting and shaping the material of which we are made, the intransigent stone of self-hood, and erecting an idealised effigy of ourselves in our own minds and in the minds of those around us and living as best we can according to its sublime example. (*G.*, p.196)

Banville here argues that we are a construction of ourselves; our minds construct our image in interaction with the Other, just as occurs with art. Banville likes "cold and pure" art and that is why he is attracted by the minds of the scientists, by the principles that rule Mathematics and Science in general. According to him, B. Russell said, "*Mathematics rightly viewed possesses not only truth but supreme beauty - a beauty cold and austere, like that of sculpture*".[15]

---

[14]In: James A.W. Heffernan (ed.) *Space, Time, Image, Sign. Essays on Literature and the Visual Arts*. p.1.
[15]Lavinia Greacen, "A Serious Writer". In: *The Irish Times*, 24 March, 1981. p.8.

I have already argued that, on the level of the narrative, Watteau's technique is reproduced in a tense equilibrium between the comic and the despairing, giving balance to life and art from different perspectives and with the detail that is typical of the French *Rococo*. However, surrealist discourse predominates throughout *Ghosts* as though it were a cry of the mind becoming its own centre, interacting with dreams and constructed reality, producing intertextual meanings from the presence of other canonised works such as *Alice in Wonderland, The Tempest, Dr. Faustus,* Nabokov's novels, and philosophical essays. The dreams show the infinite flux of wisdom. If the implicit order represents an infinite source of information, perhaps it is order itself that is the origin of this wider source of knowledge. Perhaps dreams are the bridge between a non-manifested order and the perceived one and they represent a natural transformation of the implicit within the explicit. The whole book narrates the dreams of the characters, particularly those of the narrator, and the narrative makes use of a dislocation commonly attributed to dreams. The narrator always finds himself in a composite world of shadows, phantoms and reality, on the threshold between sleep and waking – in vigil:

> ... and was convinced I had not been dreaming at all, but remembering. ...
> Certain dreams do that, they seem to darken the very air, crowding it with the shadows of another world.
> Dreams bring remembrance, too; perhaps that is what they are for, to force us to dredge up those dirty little deeds and dodges we thought we had succeeded in forgetting. These half-involuntary memories are a terrible thing. (*G.*, p.90)

In this way, Banville succeeds in illuminating the shadows and the phantoms that invade the mind of the narrator and of the very writer when he is in the process of creation. Banville questions the concept of the representation of reality through art: but, what "reality" is this? the one constructed by our minds? Ghosts and the presence of twins are powerful metaphors for the act of fiction – "*in telling a story the writer too becomes someone else*",

> ...asserting a separate identity is a powerful metaphor for the act of fiction: in telling a story the writer too becomes someone else. But it goes much deeper than that. . . . It is something that means very much to me. I suppose it is the divided self that everyone feels.[16]

This quotation is important because it also represents Banville's new worldview, suggesting that his "new synthesis" might be based on the holographic image and visualised through the mediation of the narrator, as was discussed at the beginning of my analysis of the trilogy. However, there are some contradictory events – *"But nothing is complete, and nothing whole"* - when the narrator questions scientific reality in the vortices of thought and in the flux of life:

> I suppose that is why deep down I have never been able fully to believe in reality as it is described by the science of physics, with its moments of motionless and lucid insight, as if it could be possible to take a cross-section of the moving world and put it between glass slides and study it in perfect stillness and silence. No, no, flux and flow, unstoppable, that's all there is; it terrifies me to think of it. Yet more terrifying still is the thought of being left behind. Talk is one way of keeping up. Is that not what I'm doing? If I were to stop I'd stop. (*A.*, p.71)

Only when the reader of *Athena* discovers that the names of the fictional Dutch painters, who were the authors of the pictures analysed by the narrator, are only anagrams of the name John Banville, is the writer's irony perceived. Banville assumes parodically the authorship of the fake paintings to reveal that, from the outset, they are constructions of the minds of the painter, the observer and the writer as well. The act of seeing activates his mind and gives meaning to the pictures, quite apart from the author's cynicism in relation to any values that they might contain or to the cash that might result from commercial demand. The name of one of the fictional painters refers to the name of a German painter Hans Holbein (1497-1543), but the dates of birth and death do not correspond to those of the historical painter, thus showing that we are in the field of fiction and that,

---

[16]"Out of Chaos Comes Order". In: *The Sunday Tribune*, 14 Sep., 1986. pp.18-19.

whether inside or outside it, reality will always be a construction of our mind in interaction with the external context.

The description of each picture is also a reflection on the art of writing, whether explicit or implicit in the writer's language: *"As always, Livelb adapts his vision to the dictates of available form"*.

When the narrator describes "Syrinx Delivered", he focuses on the static and sculptural image of the nymph as a way of apprehending the work of art and he quotes Adorno:

> 'In their relation to empirical reality works of art recall the theologumenon that in a state of redemption everything will be just as it is and yet wholly different.' (*A.*, p. 105)

He ends with the ironic phrase: *"I haven't even a reed pipe to play on in commemoration of you"*.

Auerbach's voice is also heard, *"In this painted world all time is eternally present and redeemable"* (*A.*, p.42), together with the voice of other anonymous critics, transforming intertextuality into the constructive method of narrative.

In the painting "Pygmalion" (called "Pygmalion and Galatea"), Banville describes the painter Belli as referring to himself in a self-criticism of his art, *"He is an anachronistic, perhaps even faintly absurd figure, displaced and out of step with his time, an exile in an alien land"* (75).

Banville's work is marked by the qualities of introspection and isolation that distance him from the already known, the familiar, approximating him to a lost and abandoned time. "The theme of death" or *"as a critic calls it 'life-in-death'"* is manifested in the morbid selection of the theme and in the obsessive pursuit of stagnation, and Banville becomes ironic in his self-criticism when he mentions that the adjective "Gothic" was wrongly applied to his work:

> His concern with the theme of death (...) is manifest in the obsessive pursuit of stillness, poise, and a kind of unearthly splendour; a pursuit which, paradoxically, imparts to his work a restless, hectic quality, so that the

epithet most often applied to it - inaccurately, of course - is 'Gothic'. (*A.*, p.76)

Banville has acknowledged many characteristics in the construction of his narrative: his determination to avoid sentimentalism, the construction of a self-contained work through self-references, and the numerous comments in parenthesis reaffirming that nothing is certain and everything suffers in the apprehension of meanings. The different voices of the narrator become echoes of his multiple selves, of the transformation into aesthetic discourse, of the discourses of current society and of the seventeenth and eighteenth centuries to which the paintings belong. All these characteristics reveal Banville's self-affirmation in his work and the search for an art that is atemporal and non-local which is manifested in the purity of form and expression: *"too self-conscious, too deliberate in its striving for pure beauty"* (76).

CLOSING REFLECTIONS
MIRRORS AND HOLOGRAPHIC LABYRINTHS

> I have frequently dreamt, for example, that I am trapped in a room. I try to get out. But I find myself back in a room. Is it the same room? I asked myself. Or am I escaping into an outer room? Or returning into an inner one? . . . This dream provided me with the motif of the maze or labyrinth which occurs so often in my fictions. I am also obsessed by a dream in which I see myself in a looking glass with several masks or faces each superimposed on the other; I peel them off successively and address the face before me in the glass; but it doesn't answer, it cannot hear me or doesn't listen, impossible to know."
>
> Jorge Luis Borges[1]

My analysis of Banville's "new aesthetic synthesis" has demonstrated the writer's constant self-evaluation. He is not a popular writer, though his concern has always been that as wide a public as possible should read his books. In my opinion, his novels are hermetic; he selects difficult words, and his narratives are dense and somewhat impermeable due to their constant self-referentiality, becoming poetic at times. The greatest success of his art lies in his creative use of language and his manipulation of discourses, which have enabled him to formulate the aesthetic synthesis which contemplates the whole in multiplicity, which has been the subject of this book. Banville has renewed the theory of the novel, crossing the frontiers of literature and interacting openly with other fields of knowledge which have been influential in former historical periods. In this renewal his tetralogy represents the summit of his achievement. According to him, in "In the Beginning were the Words", *"someone has to protect language against the depredations of politics and commerce, and, indeed, of academe"*, and if poets and novelists alone are the guardians of language they must not be conservatives:

> On the contrary, surely they should be pushing language to its limits, for it is only by risk that language lives fully, constantly renewing itself in the face of challenge. The writer must press down hard on every line, with such force and passion and attentiveness that the words begin to glow, to blush, in the sudden light of awareness. This is a dangerous way to write (especially if one is writing in Hiberno-English), but it is better to be drunk on words than sober in the safety of a grey style.[2]

Banville pushes his art to its limits, inviting his reader to cross the frontiers together with him in his search for new bifurcations and avenues on the journey.

Various images of the process of writing may be perceived through a critical reading of his novels. It may be seen as a spiral in which there is a perpetual return, though on higher planes. The end of the trilogy "closes" the "open circle" of the process in formation, on an atemporal and non-local plane which, in its turn, opens new ways for future processes. Although the luminous closures point to the different levels of the process, Banville's diversity in the use of various systems of knowledge – metafiction, science and painting interacting with history and psychoanalysis – subject the reader to an apparent chaos generated by the plurality of meanings.

The play of light produced by the mirrors of the various systems which Banville used as models in the process of representing reality, creates a multiplicity of images which seem in fact to be the reflections of different objects because the observer does not see what is producing them. Nevertheless, they belong to the

---

[1] "Joyce and Borges: Modernism and The Irish Mind" (Richard Kearney and Seamus Heaney in conversation with Jorge Luis Borges). In: R. Kearney, *Transitions*, pp. 55-56.

[2] J. Banville. "In the beginning were the words". *Weekend Guardian*, July 7-8, 1990. p. 20.

single entity that generated them. We generally perceive things in apparent disorder. According to Fritjof Capra in *The Turning Point*, order is so indefinite that it reveals itself as chance.

In order to reveal the order underlying the diversity of concepts I have presented in this study, it might be interesting at this point to re-read the process "synthetically".

Banville's literary discourse lies on the border between two genres, the novel and critical theory. His narratives result in transformations and renew the principles of nineteenth-century realism. He uses a metafictional autobiographical discourse to question the past, and to denounce the "failure" of memory and the artifice of linearity in History and Logic, thus rebutting Positivism and the Cartesian conception of the world. His discontinuous narratives thus break down formerly accepted syntheses and destabilise the structure of a system that took the form of an *imaginary materialism* based on images of the existence of an origin and on the logical development of an identity in conflict with the historical present. Banville has sought his "new synthesis" in the use of postmodern techniques and in challenging two sacred systems – Literature and the artist. As he cannot represent the world, he instead represents the different discourses of that world, revealing diverse ideologies in a state of conflict in the formation of knowledge and of a postcolonial Irish identity. Reversing the nineteenth-century concept of reality, Banville re-presents a new, political realism, of the kind referred to by the Brazilian critic Alfredo Bosi in *Reflexões sobre a Arte* when he explains the politicisation of the artistic conscience described by Benjamin:

> Realism reveals itself to be political when an artist dedicates his entire intellectual and ethical being to the idea that art is knowledge. (*translation is mine*)[3]

---

[3] Alfredo Bosi. *Reflexões sobre a arte*. p.48. "*O realismo afirma-se como político no momento em que o artista vive, com todo o seu empenho intelectual e ético, a idéia de que arte é conhecimento.*"

It is this conviction that motivates Banville to compare the scientific and artistic creative processes. He deconstructs scientific "truths" such as epistemological metaphors and he unmasks the processes of the syntheses produced by the scientific revolutions, revealing that imagination and shape are the basis of any synthesis. Nevertheless, language itself shows the impossibility of representing physical experience and, when mathematical abstraction is seen as the only exit from this *cul-de-sac*, the vision of chaos invades the space. The fictional Copernicus places a mirror between chaos and the observer with the aim of reflecting reality, but he perceives that reality is merely the reflection of a game of appearances. As I mentioned previously, Banville proposes a systemic vision of reality which respects nature's wisdom, the illusions that it generates, the flux of time and the existence of chaos allied to the dynamics of self-organisation of thought. He sees that scientific reality is a construction of the mind, ruled by the *instinctus divinus* and, in his writing, absolute truths are substituted by a wide combination of possibilities that generate relative meanings. The limits between science and fiction overlap when dealing with the concept of reality.

The images in Copernicus's mirror and the chaos behind it not only reflect the multiplicity of reality but also fragment the observer's psyche. In order to create new meanings on this plane, Banville uses the pictorial system as a model and proves that perception is the only link between the real and its representation. In my opinion, Banville's self-referential work having deconstructed the apparent mirror images, goes on to create a hologram of the human universe by projecting beams of light onto the observed object and onto the broken mirror pieces that reflect it. When the writer's laser beam – his own thought – reaches the space where the two beams of light intersect, a tridimensional image appears which seems to be the real object. Just as an observer can walk around a holographic projection and see it from different angles and yet, upon trying to touch it, discover that nothing exists, so Banville's trilogy reveals the presence of a multiple and fragmented self which disappears into a labyrinth of possibilities every time it is about to be "touched". Reality becomes a labyrinth of multiple images which the artist's mind either turns sacred when they are reflected directly in the mirror, or transforms into dreams since they are the bridge between a non-manifested order and the perceived one.

Banville focuses on the interactive synthesis between the observer and the observed, taking the pictorial system as a model, and he analyses the transpersonal experience in which matter and consciousness become fused to reveal the whole, even if this is fragmented as in the case of a holographic plate. The presence of the multiple phantoms in the narrative reveals a third level of representation, which refers to the task of the writer, who is divided between his roles of creator and censor, between the *intuitive self* that experiences writing as a subjective act of creation and the *analytical self* that distances itself from what is written in order to be able to review it and to give it new shape. This third phase of the process of representation is contrary to the first and second phases which are, respectively, modelled on natural systems and mathematical abstractions.

Banville uses various discourses that are targeted on discerning the distinction between truth and fake (scientific, legal, historical, psychological, pictorial and mythical discourses), and he projects his laser beam onto the dark side of the human being in order to reveal the existence of a multiple *self* that questions reality in the vortices of thought and in the flux of life.

The observer moves within the labyrinth of multiplicity in which the bifurcations are graphic representations of various possibilities. If the systems in non-equilibrium are sources of order, the bifurcations which are the flux of the variables, function as the union between chaos and order. Banville's proposal is not to unite opposites at this stage in the formation of his aesthetic synthesis. He wants to transform them into non-local and atemporal elements which articulate themselves simultaneously in the space of re-creation. Thus, truth is no longer absolute, being defined instead within a situation in a multiple way. Writing can only create a mediating space when we articulate the opposites; once established, such a space enables opening and closure, chaos and order, creation and reasoning to interrelate in an enriching dialectics.

Returning now to the questions raised in my introduction, I trust I have now demonstrated that Banville's "new synthesis" in the process of "becoming" proposes an open art in which *"the most lucid awareness of the universal penetrates the most vivid representation of the particular"*, to quote Alfredo Bosi.[4] Banville's synthesis resembles Walter Benjamin's proposal of "synthetic forms" of experience and narrative. It has a self-contained quality which mirrors Iris Murdoch's image of "dryness" and, above all, it represents the different Foucauldian syntheses – *a priori* and *a posteriori* – through postmodern discourses.

Banville's aesthetic synthesis seeks to analyse the limits of representation, defending a fusion between the immobile, as represented by Philosophy (which denies chance) and the mobile, as represented by popular thought (which affirms the presence of chaos). It stands at the crossroads between "time arrested", typical of philosophy, and "time passing", typical of experience. Banville introduces his readers to an open art, which reflects upon the discontinuity of phenomena in a world that is unable to provide a unitary and definitive image of itself, as he explores the holographic labyrinths at the frontiers of imagination and perception.

---

[4] Alfredo BOSI. *Reflexões sobre a arte*, p. 47.

BIBLIOGRAPHY

I- Banville's Main Publications
Books
(1970) *Long Lankin*. Dublin,The Gallery Press, 1984.
(1973) *Birchwood*. London, Grafton Books, 1987.
(1976) *Doctor Copernicus*. London, Panther Books, 1984.
(1981) *Kepler*. London, Panther Books, 1985.
(1982) *The Newton Letter*. London, Panther Books, 1984.
(1986) *Mefisto*. London, Grafton Books, 1987.
(1989) *The Book of Evidence*. London, Secker & Warburg, 1989.
(1993) *Ghosts*. London, Secker & Warburg, 1993.
(1995) Athena. London, Secker & Warburg, 1995.

Articles and Essays
"A Talk". In: *Irish University Review*, Vol.11, N° 1, Spring 1981. pp.13-17.
"Out of the Abyss," *Irish University Review*, Vol.14, No.1, Spring 1984. p.102.
"Physics and Fiction: Order from Chaos," *The New York Times Book Review*, April 21, 1985. pp. 1, 41-42.
"Lupins and Moth-laden Nights in Rosslare," *The Irish Times*, July 18, 1989. p.11.
"In the Beginning were the Words," *Weekend Guardian*, July 7-8, 1990. p.20.
"Survivors of Joyce," Martin, Augustine (ed.) *James Joyce: The Artist and the Labyrinth*. London, Ryan, 1990. pp.73-81.

Interviews
Banville, John. "An Interview with Salman Rushdie," *The New York Review of Books*, March 4, 1993. pp.34-36.
Battersby, Eileen. "Which of the Voices is Joyce's?," *The Irish Times*, August 3, 1989. p. C6.
Bencivenga, Jim. "He's no cellblock novelist," *The Christian Science Monitor*. May 17, 1990. V82 n120 p14 7 col in.

Carty, Ciaran. "Out of Chaos Comes Order," *The Sunday Tribune*, 14 September, 1986. pp.18-19.

Greacen, Lavinia. "A Serious Writer," *The Irish Times*, March 24, 1981. p.C8.

Imhof, Rüdiger. "An Interview with John Banville. 'My Readers, That Small Band, Deserve a Rest'," *Irish University Review. A Journal of Irish Studies*, Vol.11, No.1, Spring 1981. pp.5-12.

_____. "Q.& A. with John Banville," *ILS*, Spring 1987. p.13.

Jackson, Joe. "Hitler, Stalin, Bob Dylan, RoddyDpyle ... and Me," *Hot Press*, Vol 18, N° 19. 5 October 1994.

Kellaway, Kate. "Behind the Curtains," *The Observer*, Sunday 4 April, 1993. p.59.

O'Toole, Fintan. "Stepping into the Limelight - and the chaos," *The Irish Times*, October 21, 1989.

Sheehan, Ronan. "Novelists on the Novel. Ronan Sheehan Talks to John Banville and Francis Stuart," *The Crane Bag*, 3:1 (1979). pp. 76-84.

Reviews

"*Jane Austen in Her Time* by W.A. Craik. No Real Blood," *Hibernia*. November 21, 1969. p.17.

"*A Fairly Honourable Defeat* by Iris Murdoch. Major Achievements", *Hibernia*. February 20, 1970.

"*A Winter in the Hills* by John Wain. Easy Conflicts," In: *Hibernia*. May 15, 1970. p.15.

"*Robert Ce Soir and The Revocation of the Edict of Nantes* by Pierre Klossowski. *Brazen Prison* by Stanley Middleton. *The Progress of Private Lilyworth* by Russell Braddon. Some New Novels," *Hibernia*. May 14, 1971. p.17.

"*Hermann Hesse: The First Biography* by Bernhard Zeller. *Knulp* by Hermann Hesse. Artist As Healer," *Hibernia*. 23 June, 1972.

"*Relatives* by David Plante. *The Colony* by John Bowes. *Josh Lawton* by Melvyn Bragg. Two Out of Three," *Hibernia*. 14 July, 1972.

"*Yours* by Philip Collow. *Down the Rabbit Hole* by Anthony Paul. *The Half Brother* by Ailish O'Breen. Familiar Talks," *Hibernia* September 8, 1972.

"*Passions and Ancient Days: 21 Poems by Constantine Cavafy*. Selected & Trans. by E. Keely & G. Savidid. *Zone* by Guillaume Apollinaire with an Eng. Trans. by Samuel Beckett. *The Jesse Tree* by Anne Ridler. *The Way of Life: Laotzu*. Sacred and Profane," *Hibernia*. September 22, 1972. p.11.

"*Balcony of Europe* by Aiden Higgins. Colony Of Expatriates," *Hibernia*. October 6, 1972.

"*Pasmore* by David Storey. *Meeting with a Great Beast* by Leonard Wibberley. *Wild Honey Time* by M. O'Donoghue. Storeytime," *Hibernia*. November 3, 1972.

"*Enemies, A Love Story* by Isaac Bashevis Singer. *Spring Snow* by Yukio Mishima. *Souls on Fire* by Elie Wiesel. Ghosts of Judah," *Hibernia*. December 1, 1972.

"Fabrications by Michael Ayrton. *car* by Harry Crews. *Rites of Passage* by Joanne Greenberg. Highbrows and Honkies," *Hibernia.* January 19, 1973.

"Colette, A Biography by Margaret Crosland. *The Thousand and One Mornings* by Colette. Love's Labour's Lady," *Hibernia.* February 16, 1973. p.16.

"Transparent Things by Vladimir Nabokov. Inutile Genius," *Hibernia.* May 25, 1973.

The Black Book by Laurence Durrell. *Vega and Other Poems* by Laurence Durrell. *Autobiographical Writings* by Hermann Hesse. The Hard Stuff," *Hibernia.* July 13, 1973.

"A Reader's Guide to Samuel Beckett by Hugh Kenner. *The Fiction of Samuel Beckett: Form and Effect* by Porter Abbot. *First Love* by Samuel Beckett. A New Form of Chaos," *Hibernia*, 24 August 1973.

"Interpretations and Forecasts: 1922-1972 by Lewis Mumford. Essays into Sanity," *Hibernia*, 2 Nov., 1973.

"A Russian Beauty and other stories by Vladimir Nabokov. *Nikolay Gogol* by Vladimir Nabokov. A Russian Butterfly," *Hibernia.* November 16, 1973. p.21.

"Gravity's Rainbow by Thomas Pynchon. An American Monster," *Hibernia.* December 14, 1973.

"The Obscene Bird of Night by José Donoso. *In the Middle of a Life* by Richard B. Wright. In the Monster House. In: *Hibernia.* April, 12, 1974.

"Strong Opinions by Vladimir Nabokov. Opinions Better Kept Private," *Hibernia.* June 7, 1974. p.29.

"The Midas Consequence by Michael Ayrton. Afraid To Be Clever," *Hibernia.* August 30, 1974.

"A Word Child by Iris Murdoch. *Touch the Water, Touch the Wind* by Amos Oz. *See the Old Lady Decently* by B.S. Johnson. Cracker-Barrel Philosopher," *Hibernia.* May 2, 1975.

"Look at the Harlequins! by Vladimir Nabokov. *The seven Days of Creation* by Vladimir Maximov. Bread Or Madeleines," *Hibernia.* May 30, 1975.

"Tyrants Destroyed and Other Stories by Vladimir Nabokov. *The Best American Short Stories* by Hart-Davis. *The John Collier Reader. Selected Stories* by Nadine Gordimer. A Sense Of Proportion," *Hibernia.* January 30, 1976. p.26.

"Passions And Other Stories by Isaac Bashevis Singer. *The Perfect Lady By Mistake and Other Stories* by Feng Menglong. Through the Looking-Glass," *Hibernia.* May 7, 1976. p.20.

"The Uses of Division: Unity and Disharmony in Literature by John Bayley. A Sweet Disorder," *Hibernia*, Friday, May 21, 1976. p.25.

"JR. by William Gaddis. Novelist Of Swiftian Fury," *Hibernia.* Jul 30, 1976.

"Falstaff by Robert Nye. So Stout A Gentleman," *Hibernia.* September 10, 1976.

"For to End Yet Again and Other Fizzles by Samuel Beckett.Beginnings," *Hibernia*, Friday, January 7, 1977. p.32.

"*The Abyss* by Marguerite Yourcenar. Heavenly Alchemy," *Hibernia*. February 4, 1977. p.28.

"*Dangling Man. The Victim. The adventures of Augie March. Sieze the Day. Humboldt's Gift*. All by Saul Bellow. Saul Bellow's World," *Hibernia*. March 18, 1977.

"*Villa triste* by Patrick modiano. *Lunar Caustic* by Malcolm Lowry. *Bakunin: An Invention* by Horst Bienek. Adieu Tristesse," *Hibernia*. April 1, 1977.

"*The Autumn of the Patriarch* by Gabriel García Marquez. Marquez: Fatal Lure of Action," *Hibernia*, Friday, April 29, 1977. p.21.

"*Kith* by p.H.Newby. *The Castle of Crossed Destinies* by Italo Calvino. *The Demon* by Hubert Selby. Distinctly Odd," *Hibernia*. May 13, 1977.

"*Will Shakespeare* by John Mortimer. *The Abandoned Woman* by Richard Condon. *Quiet as a Nun* by Antonia Fraser. That's Entertainment," *Hibernia*. May 27, 1977.

"*Abba Abba* by Anthony Burgess. *Peter Smart's Confessions* by Paul Bailey. *The Consul's File* by Paul Theroux. The Only Begetter," *Hibernia*. June 10, 1977. p.24.

"*Falconer* by John Cheever. *The Dead Father* by Donald Barthelme. Tortured Soul," *Hibernia*. July 8, 1977.

"*Nabokov: His Life in Part* by Andrew Field. Vladimir Nabokov," *Hibernia*. August 5, 1977. p.23.

"*October Light* by John Gardner. *A Book of Common Prayer* by Joan Didion. *Speedboat* by Renata Adler. Forms of Crisis," *Hibernia*. August 19, 1977.

"*The Spiral Ascent* by Edward Upward. Act Of Faith," *Hibernia*. September 2, 1977.

"*The Ice Age* by Margaret Drabble. *A Victim of the Aurora* by Thomas Keneally. *the Danger Tree* by Olivia Manning. *Bear* by Marian Engel. Recent Fiction," *Hibernia*. September 16, 1977. p.20.

"*Great Granny Webster* by Caroline Blackwood. *Lorenzino* by Arvin Upton. *Migrations* by Gabriel Josipovici. Recent Fiction," *Hibernia*. September 30, 1977. p.27.

"*Daniel Martin* by John Fowles. Fowles At The Crossroads," *Hibernia*. October 14, 1977.

"*The Confessions of Joseph Baisz* by Dan Jacobson. *The Farewell Party* by Milan Kundera. Parables of Evil," *Hibernia*. October 21, 1977. p.28.

"*Evidence of Love* by Shirley Ann Grau. *Injury Time* by Beryl Bainbridge. *A Note that Breaks the Silence* by Adam John Munthe. Recent Fiction," *Hibernia*, October 28, 1977. p.26.

"*After Joyce: Studies in Fiction After Ulysses* by Robert Martin Adams. *The Death of Virgil* by Hermann Broch. It Is Only A Novel," *Hibernia*, Friday, November 11, 1977. p.23.

"*Quartet in Autumn* by Barbara Pym. *Excellent Women and A Glass of Blessings* by Barbara Pym. Dear Miss Pym," *Hibernia*. November 18, 1977.

"In Praise Of Bolder Women. John Banville picks the best novels of 1977," *Hibernia*. December 9, 1977. "*Triptych* by Claude Simon. *Saint Jack* by Paul Theroux," *Hibernia*. January 6, 1978.

"*Out of Focus* by Alf Mac Lochlainn. *Tennis Players* by Ronan Sheehan. *A Land not Sown* by Brian Power. Native Talent," *Hibernia*, Friday, January 20, 1978. p.23.

"*The Life of Henry James* by Leon Edel. Monument to H.J," *Hibernia*. January 27, 1978. p.24.

"*In Between the Sheets* by Ian McEwan. *Tales from the Blue Stacks* by Robert Bernen. *The Royal Guest and Other Classical Danish Narrative*. Recent Fiction," *Hibernia*. February 3, 1978. p.21.

"*Paper Tigers: The Ideal Fictions of Jorge Luis Borges* by John Sturrock. "Enigma Variations," *Hibernia*. February 16, 1978. p.22.

"*Ackroyd* by Jules Feiffer. *Ladybird in a Loony Bin* by Ian Cochrane. *Bandicoot* by Richard Condon. Recent Fiction," *Hibernia*. March 2, 1978. p.24.

"*King-Kill* by Thomas Gavin. Grand Master," *Hibernia*. March 9, 1978. p.26.

"*In A Shallow Grave* by James Purdy. *Madder Music* by Peter de Vries. *The Thin Mountain Air* by Paul Horgan. A Cunning Artist," *Hibernia*. March 30, 1978. p.27.

"*Cesar and Augusta* by Ronald Harwood. The Little Phrase," *Hibernia* April 6, 1978.

"*The Professor of Desire* by Philip Roth. Lust for Life," *Hibernia*. 13 April, 1978.

"*Kalki* by Gore Vidal. *Success* by Martin Amis. End Game," *Hibernia*. 20 April 1978. p.21.

"*Hunt* by A. Alvarez. *Housespy* by Maureen Duffy. Action," *Hibernia*. May 4, 1978. p.14.

"*In Evil Hour* by Gabriel García Marquez. Thirst For Blood," *Hibernia*. 31 January 1980. p.14.

"*Henry James: Letters 1875-1883* Edited by Leon Edel. The Assembled Image," *Hibernia*. 24 April, 1980.

"*Stephen Hawking: A Life in Science* by Michael White & John Gribben. Master of the Universe," *The Irish Times*, Feb. 1, 1982, p.8.

"*Letter to Lord Liszt* by Martin Walser. Rise and Fall at the Denture Works," *The New York Times Book Review*. Sept.15, 1985. p.11.

"*Let Newton Be! A New Perspective on his Life and Works*. Ed. by J. Fauvel, R. Flood, M. Shortland & R. Wilson. The Flight of the Inventor," *Times Literary Supplement*. March 31, 1989. p.333.

"*Warrenpoint* by Denis Donoghue. Portrait of the Critic as a Young Man," *The New York Review of Book*. October 25, 1990. pp.48-50.

"*Amongst Women* by John McGahern. *Lies of Silence* by Brian Moore, *The Innocent* by Ian McEwan. In Violent Times," *The New York Review of Books*. December 6, 1990. pp.22-23.

"*New World Avenue and Vicinity* by Tadeusz Konwicki. *Too Loud a Solitude* by Bohumil Hrabal. *Helping Verbs of the Heart* by Peter Esterhazy. Laughter in the Dark," *The New York Review of Books*. Feb.14, 1991. pp 14-17.

"*Selected Poems* by Derek Mahon. *Madoc: A Mystery* by Paul Muldoon. Slouching Toward Bethlehem," *The New York Review of Books*. Vol xxxviii, No.10. May 30, 1991.

"*Two Lives: Reading Turgenev and My House in Umbria* by William Trevor Relics," *The New York Review of Books*. September 26, 1991. pp. 29-30.

"*Jump and Other Stories* by Nadine Gordimer. *Playing the Game* by Ian Buruma. *Asyá* by Michael Ignatieff. Winners,": *The New York Review of Books*. November 21, 1991. pp. 27-29.

"*The Gonne-Yeats Letters 1893-1938: Always Your Friend.* Treading on Dreams," *Observer*, 10 May, 1992.

"*A Landing on the Sun* by Michael Frayn. *Daughters of Albion* by A.N.Wilson. Playing House," *The New York Review of Books*. May 14, 1992. pp.43.

"*Diderot: A Critical Biography* by P.N.Furbank. "Enlightenment's leading light"," *The Irish Times*. Sat. June 13, 1992.

"*The Intellectuals and the Masses: Pride and Prejudice among the Literary Intelligentsia, 1880-1939* by John Carey. Art not for the people," *The Irish Times*. Saturday, July 18, 1992.

"*The Volcano Lover. A Romance* by Susan Sontag. By Lava Possessed," *The New York Times Book Review*. August 9, 1992. pp.1, 26-27.

"*Nohow On: Company, Ill Seen Ill Said, Worstward Ho* by Samuel Beckett. The Last Word," *The New York Review of Books*. August 13, 1992. p.17

"*Michel Foucault* by Didier Eribon. John Banville on the Life and Thought of Michel Foucault. Finding the Order of Things," *The Irish Times*, Sept. 12, 1992, p.9.

"*The Volcano Lover* by Susan Sontag," *The Irish Times*. Saturday, October 3, 1992. p.9.

"*Sex* by Madonna. Sex in the Head," *The Irish Times*. October 24, 1992. p.8.

"*All the Pretty Horses* by Cormac McCarthy. Fabled beasts on the border," *The Observer*. Sunday 4 April, 1993.

II- Books and Articles on Banville

Books

Imhof, Rüdiger. *John Banville. A Critical introduction*. Dublin, Wolfhound Press, 1989.

IRISH UNIVERSITY REVIEW. *A Journal of Irish Studies. John Banville Special Issue*. Vol.11, N°1, Spring 1981.

McMinn, Joseph. *John Banville. A Critical Study*. Dublin, Gill & Macmillan, 1991.

Articles and Essays

Cornwell, Neil. "Banville" In:_____. *The Literary Fantastic. From Gothic to Postmodernism.* N.Y., London, Harvester Wheatsheaf, 1990. pp. 172-83.

Deane, Seamus. "'Be assured I am Inventing': The Fiction of John Banville". Rafroidi, P. & Maurice Harmon (eds.) *The Irish Novel in Our Time.* Lille, 1975-76. pp. 329-338.

Imhof, Rüdiger. "John Banville's Supreme Fiction". In: *Irish University Review.* Vol.11 No.1. Spring 1981. pp.52-86.

_____."Swan's Way, or Goethe, Einstein, Banville - The Eternal Recurrence". *Études Irlandaises*, No.12, Décembre 1987, pp.113-129.

_____."German Influences on John Banville and Aidan Higgins". Zach, Wolfgang & Heinz Kosok (eds.) *Literary Interrelations: Ireland, England and the World, I: Reception and Translation;II: Comparison and Impact; III: National Images and Stereotypes.* Tübingen, Narr, 1987.

_____. "In Search of the Rosy Grail: The Creative Process in the Novels of John Banville". (to be published)

Kilroy, Thomas. "Teller of Tales". *The Times Literary Supplement.* 17 March 1972. pp. 301-302.

Lysaght, Séan. "Banville's Tetralogy: The Limits of Mimesis". *Irish University Review.* Vol.21, No.1. Spring/Summer 1991. pp.82-100.

McIlroy, Brian. "Reconstructing Artistic and Scientific Paradigms: John Banville's *The Newton Letter.* In: *MOSAIC. A Journal for the Interdisciplinary Study of Literature.* Winter V.25 (1), 1992. pp.121-33.

McMinn, Joseph. "An Exalted Naming: The Poetical Fictions of John Banville". *Canadian Journal of Irish Studies.* July 1988. 14:1. pp. 17-27.

_____. "Stereotypical Images of Ireland in John Banville's Fiction". *Eire-Ireland* 23,3, Fall 1988. pp.94-102.

Molloy, Francis. "The Search for Truth: The Fiction of John Banville". *Irish University Review.* Vol.11, No.1. Spring 1981. pp.29-51.

O'Neill, Patrick. "John Banville". *SECL Studies in English and Comparative Literature.* Ed. by M. Kenneally & Wolfgang Zach. Vol 4. *Contemporary Irish Novelists.* Rüdiger Imhoff (ed.). Tübingen, Gunter Narr Verlag, 1990. pp. 207-223.

Sheehan, Ronan. "John Banville and the music of the spheres". *The Irish Times*, Saturday, September, 1986. (Weekend 9: The Arts).

_____. The Devil You Know. In: *Image*, Sept., pp.164, 166.

Reviews

[1976] Doctor Copernicus

Deane, Seamus. In: *Irish University Review.* Spring 1977, Vol.7 N° 1, pp. 120-121.

[1981] Kepler
Allen, Walter. "The unheroic hero," *The Irish Press*, Thursday, March 19, 1981.
Greacen, Lavinia. "A Serious Writer," *The Irish Times*, Tuesday, March 24, 1981. p.8.
The New Yorker. May 9, 1983. v.59. p.134(1).
Fuller, Edmund. In: *Wail Street Journal*, May 16, 1981.
McCormmach, Russell. "He Remodeled the Cosmos," *Book Reviews*.1981. pp.10 & 12.
Moyer, Gordon. In: *Sky & Telescope*, March 1984. v67. p.233(2) *Astronomy*, Oct 1983 v11 p30(1)
Stuart, Francis. "Sweet Harmony," *The Sunday Tribune*, February 8, 1981. p.26.

[1982] The Newton Letter
White, Molly. "Taken for Patricians," *The New York Times Book Review*, July 19, 1987. v92 p.19 16 col in.
Porter, Roy. In: *History Today*, August 1982. v32. p.53(1).
White, Terence de Vere. "The Centre of the Target," *Irish Times*. Sat., May 22, 1982

[1986] Mefisto
Allen, Findlay. "An Irish Devil," *The Literary Review*.
Boaz, Amy. *The New York Times Book Review*, Feb 25, 1990. p.24 6, col in.
Imhoff, Rüdiger. *Irish University Review*, Vol 17, No.1 Spring 1987. pp.137-140.
Kelly, William. "John Banville's Great Expectations," *ILS*, Spring, 1987. p.15.
Leland, Mary. "Gabriel's Sinister Angel," *The Irish Times*, Sat, September 13, 1986. (Weekend 5).

[1989] The Book of Evidence
LIBRARY JOURNAL. March 1, 1990
Abeel, Erica. *"He killed her Because He Could,"* *The New York Times Book Review*, April 15, 1990. p.11 18 col in. p.113(1)
Kenneth Mintz. *Library Journal*, March 1, 1990 v115 n4
Bawer, Bruce. "Sex and Self-Deception: A Murderer's Life," *The Wall Street Journal*, April 6, 1990. p.A17(W) pA17(E) 16 col in.
Bayley, John. "The Real Thing," *The New York Review of Books*, May 17, 1990. v37 n8. p.6 (2)
Bernstein, Richard. "Once more admired than bought, a writer finally basks in success," *The New York Times*, May 15, 1990. v139 pC13(L) 27 col in.
Craig, Patricia. "After such knowledge," *Times Literary Supplement*, March 31, 1989. n4487. p.344(1).
Cryer, Dan. "The Mind of a Murderer Untroubled by Guilt," *The Irish Times*.

D'Evelyn, Thomas. "Murder with and without Mystery," *The Christian Science Monitor*, May 17, 1990 v82 n120 p14 21 col in.
Prescott, Peter. "Inside the Mind of a Murderer," *Newsweek*, April 23, 1990. v115 n17. p.71 (1).
Steinberg, Syhil. *Publishers Weekly*, Feb 9, 1990 v237 n6. p.44(1).
Taylor, Robert. "'Evidence' traces a man's descent into evil," *The Boston Globe*, Wednesday, 1990. p.46.

[1993] Ghosts
Eder, Richard. "Raskolnikov on the Couch," *FanFare*, Sunday, November 7, 1993. p.35
Hand, Derek. "Nearly a Novel," *ILS*, Fall 1993. p.7.
Kellaway, Kate. "Behind the curtains," *The Observer*, 4 April, 1993. p.59.
Korn, Eric. "An Innocent Isle," *TSL. The Times Literary Supplement*, April 9, 1993. n4697 p.20 (1)
Whiteside, Shaun. "Shadow Plays," *New Stateman and Society*, April 16, 1993. v6 n248. p.41(1).

III- Secondary Sources

On the Novel
Acheson, James (ed.) *The British and the Irish Novel Since 1960*. London: Macmillan, 1991.
Bakhtin, M.M. *The Dialogic Imagination*. Austin: University of Texas Press, 1981
Benjamin, Walter. "O narrador", In: Benjamin, W. *Obras Escolhidas. Magia e Técnica, Arte e Política*. São Paulo: Editora Brasiliense, 1986.
Bradbury, Malcolm. *The Social Context of Modern English Literature*. Oxford: Basil Blackwell, 1971.
_____. (ed.) *The Novel Today*. Great Britain: Fontana Paperbacks, 1977.
_____ & David Palmer (eds.) *The Contemporary English Novel*. London: Edward Arnold, 1979.
Cronin, John. *The Anglo-Irish Novel*. New Jersey: Barnes & Noble Books, 1980.
Daiches, David. *The Present Age in British Literature*. Bloomington London: Indiana University Press, 1969.
Derrida, Jacques. *Writing and Difference*. London: Routledge & Kegan Paul, 1981
Fraser,G.S. *The Modern Writer and his World*. Harmondsworth, England: Penguin Books, 1972.
Harmon, Maurice. "Generations Apart: 1925-1975". In: Rafroidi, Patrick & M. Harmon, M. (eds.) *The Irish Novel in Our Time*, Publications de l'Universite de Lille III et C.E.R.S.U.L., 1975- 6. pp. 49-65.
_____. "First impressions: 1968-78". In: Rafroidi, P. & T. Brown. *The Irish Short Story*. France: University de Lille III, 1979. pp. 63-77.

_____ & Roger Mc Hugh. *Short History of Anglo-Irish Literature. From its origin to the present day*. Dublin: Wolfhound Press, 1982.
Hazell, Stephen (ed.) *The English Novel. Developments in Criticism since Henry James*. London: Macmillan, 1978.
Josipovici, Gabriel (ed.) *The Modern English Novel. The reader, the writer and the work*. London: Open books, 1976.
Karl, Frederick R. *A reader's Guide to the Contemporary English Novel*. (Revised Edition). London: Thames & Hudson, 1972.
Kemp, Peter. "British Fiction of the 1980s". In: Bradbury, M. & Judy Cooke (eds.) *New Writing*. London: Minerva & the British Council, 1992. pp.216-228.
Lukács, Georges. *La Théorie du roman*. Paris: Gonthier, 1963.
Lodge, David. "The Novelist Today: Still at the Crossroads?". In: Bradbury, M. & Judy Cooke (eds.) *New Writing*. London: Minerva & the British Council, 1992. Pp.203-215.
Rafroidi, P. & T. Brown. *The Irish Short Story*. France: University de Lille III, 1979.
Scholes, R. & Kellogg, R. *A Natureza da Narrativa*. São Paulo: Editora McGraw-Hill do Brasil, 1977.
Stevenson, Randall. *The British Novel since the Thirties. An Introduction*. London: B.T. Batsford Ltd., 1986.
Stevick, Philip (ed.). *The Theory of the Novel*. New York: The Free Press, 1967.
Watt, Ian. *The Rise of the Novel*. G.Britain: Harmondsworth, The Penguin Books, 1968.
Zola, Emilio. *La Escuela Naturalista. Estudios Literarios*, trans. Alvaro Yunque. Buenos Aires: Editorial Futuro, 1945.

On Postmodernism and Postcolonialism

Adam, Ian & Helen Tiffin. (eds.) *Past. The Last Post. Theorizing Post-Colonialism and Post-Modernism*. New York, Harvester Wheatsheaf, 1991. 213 p.
Bhabha, Homi K. (Ed.) *Nation and Narration*. London: Routledge, 1990.
_____. "Signs Taken for Wonders: Questions of Ambivalence and Athority under a Tree Outside Delhi," May 1817. In: *Critical Inquiry*, Autumn 1985. pp.143-165.
_____. "Interrogating Identity. Frantz Fanon and the post-colonial prerogative". In: *The Location of Culture*.1994.pp.40-65.
_____. "The other question: difference, discrimination and the discourse of colonialism". In: Barker, F. *et alii*. (eds.) *Literature, Politics and Theory*. London: Methuen, 1986. pp.149-172.
Coelho, Teixeira. *Moderno Pós Moderno*. São Paulo: L & PM Editores, 1986.
Foster, Hal (ed.) *Postmodern Culture*. London & Sydney, Pluto Press, 1987.
Hassan, Ihab. *The postmodern Turn. Essays in Postmodern Theory and Culture*. Columbus, Ohio State University Press, 1987.

Hutcheon, Linda. *The Poetics of Postmodernism*. London: Routledge, 1988
_____. *The Politics of Postmodernism*. London: Routledge,1989.
Kearney, Richard. *Transitions. Narratives in Modern Irish Culture*. Manchester: Manchester University Press, 1988.
Lodge, David. (1977) "Postmodernist Fiction". In: *the Modes of Modern Writing. Metaphor, Metonymy, and the Typology of Modern Literature*. London: Edward Arnold, 1989.
Lyotard, Jean-François. *O Pós-Moderno*, trans. Ricardo Corrêa Barbosa. Rio de Janeiro: José Olympio Editora, 1988.
McHale, Brian. *Postmodernist Fiction*. London & N.York: Routledge, 1987.
Menezes de Souza, L. M. "O rato que ruge: o discurso crítico-literário póscolonial como suplemento. In: *Crop*. N°1. São Paulo: FFLCH-USP, 1994. pp.60-66.
Norris, Christopher. *What's Wrong with Postmodernism. Critical theory and the ends of philosophy*. New York: Harvester Wheatsheaf, 1990.
Salusinszky, Imre. *Criticism in Society*. New York & London: Methuen, 1987.
Subirats, Eduardo. *Da Vanguarda ao Pós-Moderno*. São Paulo: Livraria Nobel S.A., 1986.
Taylor, Mark C. (ed.) *Deconstruction in Context. Literature and Philosophy*. Chicago & London: The University of Chicago Press, 1986.
Thiher Allen. *Words in Reflection. Modern Language Theory and Postmodern Fiction*. Chicago & London: The University of Chicago Press, 1984.
Waugh, Patricia. *Metafiction. The Theory and Practice of Self-Conscious Fiction*. London & N.York: Methuen, 1984.

On Science and Literature

Amrine, Frederick (ed.) *Literature and Science as Modes of Expression*. Dordrecht/Boston/London: Kluwer Academic Publishers, 1989.
ANNALS OF SCHOLARSHIP. Metastudies of the Humanities and Social Sciences. Vol 4, Number 1, Fall 1986. *Science and the Imagination*. ed. by G.S. Rousseau.
Arnold, Mathew. "Literature and Science" from *Discourses in America* (lecture 2), 1883-1884. In: Cadden, John & Brostowin, P.R.(eds.) *Science and Literature. A Reader*. Boston: D.C.Heath & Co., 1964; pp.15-23.
Barthes, Roland. (1984) *The Rustle of Language*. Berkeley & L.A., University of California Press, 1989.
Beer, Gillian. *Arguing with the Past. Essays in narrative from Woolf to Sidney*. London & New York: Routledge, 1989. 206 p.
_____. (1983) *Darwin's Plots. Evolutionary Narrative in Darwin, George Eliot and Nineteenth-Century Fiction*. London: Ark Paperbacks, 1985.
Bulhof, Ilse N. *The Language of Science. A Study of the Relationship between Literature and Science in the perspective of a Hermeneutical Ontology*. Leiden, N.Y. Köln, E.J.Brill, 1992.

Cadden, John J. & Brostowin, Patrick R. (eds.). *Science and Literature. A Reader.* Boston: D.C.Heath & Co., 1964.
Capra, Fritjof. *The Turning Point. Science, Society and the Rising Culture.* N.Y.: Bantam Books, 1983.
_____. [1982] *O Ponto de Mutação. A Ciência, a Sociedade e a Cultura emergente,* trans. Álvaro Cabral. São Paulo: Editora Cultrix, 1993-97.
Chapple, J.A.V. *Science and Literature in the 19th Century.* London: Macmillan, 1986.
Coracini, Maria José. *Um Fazer Persuasivo. O Discurso Subjetivo da Ciência.* São Paulo: Pontes & EDUC, 1991.
DAEDALUS. Journal of the American Academy of Arts and Sciences. Art and Science, Vol.115, Number 3, Summer 1986.
Dale, Peter Allan. *In Pursuit of Scientific Culture. Science, Art and Society in the Victorian Age.* Madison, University of Wisconsin Press, 1989.
Davie, Donald. *The Language of Science and the Language of Literature, 1700-1740.* London & N.Y., Sheed & Ward, 1963.
ET CETERA. Winter 1985.
GALILEU GALILEI. Diálogo sobre os dois máximos sistemas do mundo Ptolomaico e Copernicano. Trad. Letizio Mariconda e Pablo Rubén Mariconda. São Paulo: 1990 (no prelo).
Garwin & Heath, James M. *Bucknell Review. Science and Literature.* London & Toronto: Bucknell Univ. Press, 1983.
Guthke, Karl S. (1983) *The Last Frontier. Imagining Other Worlds, from the Copernican Revolution to Modern Science Fiction.* Ithaca & London: Cornell Univ. Press, 1990.
Harrison, Tony. *Square Rounds.* London, Faber & Faber, 1992.
Hayles, N. Katherine. *The Cosmic Web. Scientific Field Models & Literary Strategies in the 20th. Century.* Ithaca & London: Cornell University Press, 1984.
_____. *Chaos Bound. Orderly Disorder in Contemporary Literature and Science.* Ithaca & London: Cornell University Press, 1990. 309 p.
_____. (ed.) *Chaos and Order. Complex Dynamics in Literature and Science.* Chicago & London: The University of Chicago Press, 1991.
Hofstadter, Douglas R. *Metamagical Themas. Questing for the Essence of Mind and Pattern.* N.Y: Basic Book, Inc. Publishers, 1945.
_____. *Gödel, Escher, Bach: An Eternal Golden Braid.* N.Y., Vintage Books, 1980.
Huxley, Aldous. *Literature and Science.* N.Y. & London: Harper and Row Publishers, 1963.
A JOURNAL of Literature, Science and technology, Vol 1 Number 2, Spring 1993. The John Hopkins University Press.
Keller, Evelyn Fox. *Reflections on Gender and Science.* New Haven & London: Yale University Press, 1985.

Koestler, Arthur. *The Sleepwalkers. A History of man's changing vision of the Universe*. London: Hutchinson, 1959..

Kuhn, Thomas. *The Essential Tension. Selected Studies in Scientific Tradition and Change*. Chicago & London: The Univ. of Chicago Press, 1977.

_____. (1957) *The Copernican Revolution. Planetary Astronomy in the Development of Western Thought*. Cambridge, Mass. & London: Harvard University Press, 1977.

Pécheux, Michael & Fichant, Michael. *Sobre a História das Ciências*. São Paulo: Edições Mandacaru Ltda., 1989.

Peterfreund, Stuart (ed.) *Literature and science. Theory and Practice*. Boston (U.S.): Northeastern University Press, 1990.

Prigogine, Ilya & Stengers, Isabelle. *Order out of Chaos. Man's new dialogue with nature*. London, Flamingo, 1984.

PTOLEMY, COPERNICUS, KEPLER. Chicago, London: Encyclopaedia Britannica Great Books, No. 16. 1085 p.

Reichenbach, Hans. *From Copernicus to Einstein*, trans. Ralph B. Winn. New York: Dover Publications, Inc., 1980.

Slade, Joseph & Judith Yaross Lee (eds.) *Beyond the Two Cultures: Essays on Science, Technology and Literature*. Iowa: Iowa State University Press, 1990.

STUDIES IN LITERATURE, Vol. 19, Number 1, 1987. University of Hartford.

Talbot, Michael. [1991] *O Universo Holográfico*, trans. Maria de Fátima S.M. Marques. São Paulo: Editora Best Seller, s.d.

Wightman, W.P.D. *Science in a Renaissance Society*. London: Hutchinson University Library, 1972.

On Fine Arts and Literature

Bosi, Alfredo. *Reflexões sobre a arte*. São Paulo: Editora Ática S.A., 1986.

Chipp, Herschel B. [1968] *Teorias da Arte Moderna*, trans. Waltensir Dutra *et alii*. São Paulo: Martins Fontes, 1988.

Elsen, Albert E. (1969) *Los Propósitos del Arte. Introducción a la historia y a la apreciación del arte*, trans. Maria del Pilar Ganose de Altabella. Madrid: Aguilar, 1971.

Garland, Hamlin. *Crumbling Idols. Twelve Essays on Art Dealing Chiefly with Literature, Painting and the Drama*. Cambridge, Massachusetts: The Belknag Press of Harvard Univ. Press, 1960.

Gowing, Lawrence. *Vermeer*. London, Faber & Faber, s.d.

Hagstrum, Jean H. *The Sister Arts. The Tradition of Literary Pictorialism and English Poetry from Dryden to Gray*. Chicago: The University of Chicago Press, 1958.

Hale, Philip L. *Jan Vermeer of Delft*. Boston: Small, Maymard & Co., 1913.

Hatzfeld, Helmut. *Literature through Art. A New Approach to French Literature*. N.York: Oxford University Press, 1952.
Heffernan, James A. W. (ed.) *Space, Time, Image, Sign. Essays on Literature and the Visual Arts*. New York: Peter Lang, 1987.
Johnson, Lee McKay. *The Metaphor of Painting. Essays on Baudelaire, Ruskin, Proust and Pater*. Michigan: UMI Research Press, 1980.
Jones, Louisa E. *Pierrot-Watteau. A Nineteenth-Century Myth*. Paris: Gunter Narr Verlag. Tübingen Editions Jean-Michel Place, 1984.
Michel, Marianne Roland. *Watteau. An Artist of the 18th. Century*. N.Y.: Alpine Fine Arts Collection Ltd., 1984.
Nunes, Benedito. *Introdução à Filosofia da Arte*. São Paulo, Editora Ática, 1989,
Pickering, F.P. *Literature and Art in the Middle Ages*. Florida, University of Miami Press, 1970.
Praz, Mario. *Mnemosyne. The Parallel between Literature and the Visual Arts*. U.S.A.: Princeton University Press, 1970.
Stein, Leo. *Appreciation: Painting, Poetry and Prose*. N.Y., Crown Publishers, 1947.
Steiner, Wendy. *The Colors of Rhetoric. Problems in the Relation between Modern Literature and Painting*. Chicago & London: The University of Chicago Press, 1982.
_____. *Pictures of Romance. Form against Context in Painting and Literature*. Chicago & London: The University of Chicago Press, 1988.

Other Works
Barker, A.J.[1973] *Irlanda Sangrenta*, trans. Edmond Jorge. Rio de Janeiro: Editora Renes Ltda., 1979..
Benjamin, Walter. *Obras Escolhidas. Magia e Ténica, Arte e Política*, trans.. Sergio Paulo Rouanet. São Paulo: Editora Brasiliense, 1985.
Brown, Terence. *Ireland. A Social and Cultural History 1922-1985*. London: Fontana Press, 1981.
Cairns, David & Shaun Richards. *Writing Ireland. Colonialism, nationalism and culture*. Manchester: Manchester University Press, 1988.
Coogan, Tim Pat. (ed.) *Ireland and the Arts*. London: The Literary Review, s.d.
Deane, Seamus. *A Short History of Irish Literature*. London, Hutchinson, 1986.
Derrida, Jacques. *Writing and Difference*. London & Henley: Routledge & Kegan Paul, 1981.
_____. *Positions*. Chicago: The University of Chicago Press, 1981
_____. *The Ear of the Other. Otobiography, Transference, Translation*, trans. Peggy Kamuf.. Lincoln & London: University of Nebraska Press, 1985. 185 p.
Foster, R.F. *Modern Ireland 1600-1972*. London: Penguin Books, 1988.
Foucault, Michel. [1969] *A arquelogia do Saber*, trans. Luiz Felipe Baeta Neves. Rio de Janeiro: Forense-Universitária, 1987.

_____ [1966] *As palavras e as coisas. Uma arquelogia das ciências humanas*, trans. Salma Tannus Muchail. São Paulo: Livraria Martins Fontes Editora Ltda., 1985.

_____. *Politics, Philosophy, Culture. interviews and other writings 1977-1984.* (1988) Introduction by Lawrence Kritzman. New York & London: Routledge, 1990..

Herrnstein Smith, Barbara. *Contingencies of Value. Alternative Perspectives for Critical Theory.* Cambridge, Mass. & London: Harvard University Press, 1988.

IRISHNESS IN A CHANGING SOCIETY. (Ed. The Princess Grace Irish Library, Monaco). Gerrards Cross: Colin Smythe, 1988.

Izarra, Laura. "James Stephens. *The Demi-Gods* at the Crossroads." Diss., Brazil U, 1988.

Kearney, Richard. Poetics of Imagining. From Husserl to Lyotard. London: Harper Collins Academic, 1991.

_____. *The Irish Mind. Exploring Intellectual Traditions.* Dublin: Wolfhound Press, 1985.

_____. (ed.) *Across the Frontiers. Ireland in the 1990's.* Dublin: Wolfhound Press, 1988.

Kirby, Peadar. *Has Ireland a Future?.* Cork & Dublin: The Mercier Press, 1988. 139 p.

Mansergh, Nicholas. *The Irish Question 1840-1921.* Toronto: University of Toronto Press, 1975.

OS PENSADORES: BRUNO. VICO, Helda Barraco e Nestor Deola. São Paulo: Nova Cultural, 1988.

Quine, W.V. *Pursuit of TRUTH.* Cambridge, Mass. & London: Harvard University Press, 1990.

Riffaterre, Michael. *Fictional Truth.* London, The Johns Hopkins University Press, 1990.

Rossett, Clément. [1971] *Lógica do pior,* trans. Fernando J. Fagundes Ribeiro e Ivana Bentes Rio de Janeiro: Espaço e Tempo, 1989.

Said, Edward. *Culture and Imperialism.* London: Vintage,1993.

_____. Orientalism. London: Routledge & Kegan Paul, 1978.

Schaff, Adam. (1971) *História e Verdade,* trans. Maria P. Duarte. São Paulo: Martins Fontes, 1987.

Silveira, Tasso. *Literatura Comparada.* Rio de Janeiro: Editora GRD, 1964.

Tieghen, Paul van. *La Littérature Comparée.* Paris: Librarie Armand Colin, 1951.

Toffler, Alvin. *The Third Wave.* Trans. João Távora. *A Terceira Onda.* Rio de Janeiro: Editora Record. n.d. .

Veeser, H. Aram (ed.) *The New Historicism.* London: Routledge, 1989.

Wellek, R. "The Name and Nature of Comparative Literature". In: *Discriminations.* New Haven: Yale University, 1970.

INDEX

Arnold, M., 56
autobiography & the novel, 12, 25, 65, 79, 129
Bhabha, H., 20, 30, 38
Bakhtin, M., 22,
Banville
  Athena, 7, 12, 127, 129, 136, 143-156
  Birchwood, 7,11,18-19, 25,27, 29-48, 50, 66, 73, 99, 113, 114, 116, 127, 146, 148
  The Book of Evidence, 7, 127, 129-135, 137, 140, 143, 145, 147, 148, 151
  Doctor Copernicus, 7, 8, 12, 54, 61-80, 95, 105, 112, 160
  Ghosts, 7,, 12, 48, 127, 129, 132, 135-143, 147-149, 153
  Kepler, 7, 8, 12, 54, 58-59, 74-76, 80-96, 106, 109-110, 112, 122, 125
  Long Lankin, 7
  Mefisto, 7, 12, 54, 58-59, 75, 107, 113-123, 125, 139, 146
  The Newton Letter, 7, 12, 18-19, 54, 58, 74, 75, 95, 97-107, 109, 110, 112, 143

Nightspawn, 7, 10-11, 18-28, 49, 66, 73, 127, 148
Barthes, 56
Benjamin, W., 13, 40, 105, 159, 162
biography & fiction, 10, 57, 65, 79, 95, 98-99, 103
Bosi, A., 159, 162
Borges, J.L., 1, 14, 125, 157, 158
Bradbury, M., 1
Capra, F., 107, 112, 159
chance, 55, 87, 111, 113-125
chaos, 2, 3, 6, 11, 13, 18, 24, 25, 28, 34, 35, 45, 47, 53, 55-56, 59, 61, 68-70, 75-76, 80, 87, 90, 92, 94, 100, 107, 109-114, 118-121, 123-125, 127, 134, 137, 139, 147, 152, 154, 158, 160-162
commedia dell'arte, 139, 141, 142
Deane, S., 9, 31,
Derrida, J., 23, 25
Descartes, 29-31, 112, 124, 159, 163
dreams, 41, 87, 92, 137, 149, 153, 161, 157
Eco, U., 58
Einstein, 7, 107, 112, 116, 117, 125
entropy, 110, 11, 113, 118, 120
Foucault, M., 5, 13-14, 27, 29-30, 47, 65, 72, 73, 77, 162

ghosts, 67, 73, 96, 119, 120, 134-139, 151, 153
Harmon, M., 8,
historiographic metafiction, 10, 57
history & fiction, 6, 14-15, 27, 31, 33, 44, 51, 57, 58, 95, 97-100, 102, 103-109, 124, 158-159
hologram, 128, 131, 133, 134, 140, 147, 154, 157, 160-162
Hutcheon, L., 3, 10, 57
Huxley, A., 56
Huxley, T.H., 56
hybridity, 44, 48, 76
identity, 3, 5, 12, 17-19, 25-27, 30, 33, 35, 37-44, 46-47, 55, 116, 127, 143, 154, 159
Imhof, R., 8-11, 18-20, 26,31, 39, 45, 64, 67, 81, 83, 90, 95, 97, 112, 114, 129
instictus divinus, 83, 90, 96, 125, 160
intertextuality, 8, 26, 31, 155, 149, 153, 155
Kearney, R., 1, 10, 31, 39, 66, 93, 158
Koestler, A., 62, 63, 64, 83, 85, 86
Kuhn, T. S., 62, 70, 71, 77
labyrinths, 19, 112, 157, 160, 161, 162
language, 2, 4-6, 8, 12, 17, 25, 27, 29, 33, 37, 42, 49, 53-56, 59, 64-67, 69-70, 74, 76, 91, 105-107, 112, 124, 148-149, 155, 157, 158, 160
McMinn, J., 8, 18-19, 32, 39, 64-65, 67, 97, 99, 114
metafiction. 2, 4, 7, 10-12, 17-19, 24, 64-65, 72, 97, 116, 122, 158, 159
Newton, 56,58,97, 98-100, 104, 110, 112, 125
novel
  autobiographical, 18, 22,
  Big House, 31, 39, 97
  biographical, 56, 57, 94
  detective, 19-20, 21, 27, 32, 45, 46
  genre, 1, 2, 4, 9-10, 12, 14, 21, 24, 32, 37, 61, 69, 75-76, 98, 112, 123, 135, 144, 148, 158
  Goethe's *Faustus*, 114
  historical allegory, 33
  19th century, 32, 48, 51
  picaresque, 32
  Proustian, 32
  self-conscious/self-contained,57-58, 64, 69, 94, 131, 156, 157, 160, 161, 162
  shape, 59, 76, 94, 95, 109-123
O'Neill, P., 9
order, 2, 5-6, 11, 13, 18, 24, 28, 34, 53-56, 58, 68-69, 80, 109-125, 127, 128, 134, 139, 147, 152-53, 154, 159, 161, 162
painting & fiction, 6, 13-14, 33, 40, 51, 63, 77, 129, 131, 132, 135, 139, 140-147, 152, 154-156, 158
(post)colonial, 3, 4, 15, 17-20, 23, 25-51, 159
postmodernism, 2, 4, 5, 6, 10-11, 13-15, 17-18, 30, 46, 54, 57, 76, 93, 106, 159, 162
Prigogine & Stengers, 6, 100, 111, 123, 125, 152
reality, 1, 6, 8-12, 17-18, 20, 31, 41, 45, 51, 53-55, 57, 59, 61, 64-67, 70-71, 75, 80, 87, 91, 92-94, 98, 106-107, 109, 11, 125, 127, 128, 133, 139, 140, 141, 145, 149, 153-155, 158, 159, 160, 161
representation (the crisis of), 1, 5-6, 11-14, 17, 54, 64, 65, 74, 93, 94, 107, 136, 146, 149, 153, 160, 161, 162
Riffaterre, M., 79, 102, 106
Rosset, C. 113, 115

Index

self/selves & the Other, 2-3, 18, 25, 27, 30, 33-34, 39, 47, 72, 78, 101, 105, 115-117, 120, 124, 129, 130, 134, 136, 137, 140, 141-142, 146, 152, 154, 157, 160, 161

self-referentiality, 8, 12, 59, 74, 114, 157, 160

shape, 11, 27-29, 59, 76, 81, 83-84, 91, 93, 94-95, 100, 109-110, 116, 160, 161

science, 4, 6, 11, 15, 53, 55, 56, 59, 61, 64-65, 68, 83-84, 86, 94, 95, 103, 109, 110, 111, 114, 158

science & fiction, 12, 14, 33, 48, 51, 53-125, 160

science fiction, 92-93

Snow, C.P., 55

synthesis, 4, 5-6, 11, 13, 18, 54, 57-59, 62, 80, 81-82, 92, 93, 94, 120, 148-152, 154, 157, 159, 161, 162

Talbot, M., 128

The Big House, 8, 31, 33, 34, 36, 39, 99, 100, 114

truth, 4, 6, 9, 12, 14, 19, 23-24, 30, 45, 53-54, 57-58, 62-64, 67-70, 72-75, 79, 80, 85, 87, 89, 94-99, 101-107, 109, 111, 121, 123-124, 127, 144, 147, 149, 150, 151, 152, 160, 161

twins (& duality), 33, 43-44, 46-47, 73, 115, 116-117, 120, 127, 146, 148, 153, 154

Vermeer, 130, 131, 133, 134, 139, 141

void, 65, 91, 95, 113, 121

vortices, 22, 134, 154, 161

Watteau, 135-137, 139-143, 152-153

Wittgenstein, L., 25, 48, 65, 66, 68-69, 74